100
WAYS
TO
MAKE
MONEY

Alison Rose

TEACH YOURSELF BOOKS

Many thanks to Tony Guy

A catalogue entry for this title is available from the British Library.

ISBN 0 340 70512 4

First published 1998
Impression number   10 9 8 7 6 5 4 3 2
Year   2002 2001 2000 1999

The 'Teach Yourself' name and logo are registered trade marks of Hodder & Stoughton Ltd.

Typeset by Transet Limited, Coventry, England.
Printed in Great Britain for Hodder & Stoughton Educational, a division of Hodder Headline Plc, 338 Euston Road, London NW1 3BH by Cox & Wyman Ltd, Reading, Berkshire.

CONTENTS

PREFACE

Right across the United Kingdom the number of small businesses being set up is on the increase, as more and more people choose to work from home. It's a phenomenon of our time, helped along by the advent of computers, modems, home fax machines, changing work patterns and society's needs for a whole new range of services.

Most new businesses start small – someone working out of a spare room (or even the dining room) of their home, using just a telephone and perhaps a computer that might be a bit the worse for wear. These small businesses may spring from a simple idea, or the desire to provide a service that no one else has thought of.

As a journalist I've discovered there are mums, dads, grandparents, young people and retired folk, all trying their hand at small businesses. The problem is often that they have the motivation and the desire to make a project work but they either lack the basic business knowledge or they don't know what type of small business would suit them. These are ordinary people who just needed ideas to help get them started.

With this in mind, I have hunted around and come up with 100 money-making schemes. These are not going to make you a millionaire overnight, and they are certainly not get-rich-quick schemes. They are simple ideas that, if nurtured, will help you earn perhaps an extra £30–50 a week – enough to pay a few extra bills. Who knows though? If you find something successful, and stick with it, it might become a full-time business.

The schemes I describe are mostly low-risk, requiring limited capital to set them up, and they can be done at home with limited training. The ideas suit a range of age groups and situations. They are fun and many of them have a contemporary twist – a unique marketing idea or concept which will make your business stand out.

The thing to remember is a small business takes time, effort and commitment if you want to make it work. It also takes business sense. That's why a key part of this book is aimed at helping you find out if you have the skills to make a business work, and providing information on how to go about setting up a business. This is vital information and you should read it – it includes details on budgeting, financial issues, insurance, tax and tips on getting a small business started. It also includes contact numbers and addresses for further guidance in setting up a small business.

To use this book successfully, read through the business section first and decide if being a small-business operator is for you. Then browse through the 100 suggested business ideas. Perhaps there is one that would suit you, or one idea might spark off another scheme of your own. Once you have selected the idea, return to the business section and use it to devise your financial plan and marketing strategy – then get started. Remember, this book is only a resource. It is you who will ultimately make the business a success.

As well as referring to the business matters section in this book, you should also consult local business associations, accountants, lawyers and government agencies for guidance in setting up your business. They are a valuable resource. Remember, the more information you have, the better prepared you will be to deal with problems.

Be sure to research your business concept thoroughly – especially the financial matters. In the UK around 400 thousand small businesses fail each year, and that's about the same number as are set up in a year. Keeping that in mind, remember that the key to a successful small business is sticking to your plan and knowing when to call it quits and try something new.

I am a great believer in seizing the day and stretching yourself and your dreams. If you have a good idea don't put it off. Go out there and give it a go. Only you can make it happen. I believe that if you plan well and do your research, your small business will be a success.

Good luck!

Alison Rose

1

GETTING STARTED

This chapter covers the basics that you need to consider before launching off into the unknown.

- Do I have what it takes to go into business on my own?
- What goals should I set myself?
- What research should I do first?
- How have other people fared?

Do I have what it takes?

Setting up a small business can be a big job. Turning an idea into a money-making scheme involves responsibility and financial risk. More than one-third of all small businesses fail in the first twelve months of operation, not because the business idea was bad but because of poor financial planning. So if you are considering setting up a small business here is a check list of requirements. Have a go at setting up a small business if you have:

- an identified market and products or services to sell to that market
- a good knowledge of the competition
- a thorough business plan, including market prices, costs and profit margins
- funds to invest in the business
- access to legal, business and sound financial advice
- a start-up date
- a list of business goals e.g. profit expectations, sales expectations

- determination to make the business work
- the ability to work long hours and handle the tough times as well as the good times
- a belief in yourself and your product or service
- a cut-off date and a contingency plan, in case the business does not work out.

If you have all – or at least most – of these then you are halfway to operating your own business.

Setting goals

It is vital when setting up a small business to set goals for yourself *and* for your business. This gives you something to strive for and also allows you to measure just how successful your venture is. The goals to consider, when you attempt to set up your own small business, include:

- deciding on a business concept and setting a start-up date for your business
- achieving your first sale
- successfully marketing your product by distributing fliers, posters and putting advertisements in papers
- rewarding yourself after the first successful three to six months of operation
- expanding your product or service base to satisfy customer demand
- using your profits to buy new equipment for your business
- turning your business from a part-time one into a full-time money-earner.

The aim is to set the goals you can achieve and reward yourself each time these goals are met. Just like careful financial planning, goal-setting allows you, as a small-business operator, to measure success and predict future business growth or slumps.

Research

The key to success in a small business is research. You *must* know your market and your customers thoroughly. You *must* seek professional guidance on legal and financial matters, as well as on government regulations. Aim to learn as much as you can about operating a small business and especially the business you choose. You may only be aiming to earn an extra £30–50 a week from your business, but that doesn't mean you should take short-cuts in finding out all you can about your venture and the possible pitfalls.

Before you start your business, talk to accountants, bank managers, lawyers and government agencies as well as small-business aid groups. Find out what they can offer you and how they can help you make your business better. Then, once you have worked out what you are going to offer, talk to potential customers. This could mean asking family and friends what they think of your concept and how they would make it better.

Go to your local shopping centre and survey shoppers. Ask them for an unbiased opinion.

If your business requires you to sell through weekend markets, set up a trial stand. Talk to people who show interest and really listen to their comments. Write them down and be as flexible as possible. The information you gather might help you to modify your product or service to make it even better.

Try to do a small business course at your adult education college. These courses are normally four to eight weeks long and sessions are held once a week. The information you will learn will be invaluable.

Always check with your local authority to find out if there are any laws relating to your product or service.

———————— Success stories ————————

Just getting your business up and running is a tough job, but there are rewards, as you will see from the following small business success stories.

These people have all been through the same process on which you are about to embark. They started with a simple idea and turned it into a money-making scheme. Along the way, some encountered criticism and all experienced problems but they stuck with it because they were passionate about their work and their business. If you do the same, hopefully you can enjoy success as they have.

✓✓✓ *Loads of dough*

For twelve years 41-year-old Marlene Meadon worked for a gaming company in Swansea. But during that time she harboured a dream to run her own business. Then four years ago Marlene realised her small business success could literally be on her doorstep.

'I lived on the edge of the Swansea Enterprise Park,' explains Marlene. 'I noticed there were various sandwich delivery trucks serving the several thousand people who worked there but they had no proper access to catering facilities. However, those delivery trucks seemed to disappear as fast as they appeared. The operators were largely un-reliable and customers never knew when the vans would arrive.'

So Marlene did some research and found there was a market for a fast-food delivery service that provided hygienic facilities, a choice of products and was reliable.

'I felt that if the people working in the Park could rely on regular deliveries they wouldn't have to make their own food to bring to work, but rather would buy from me,' says Marlene.

So this former employee took the plunge and became her own boss. Marlene knew she had to set up her business with limited capital, and she needed to make her clients understand she was different from the previous unreliable traders. She did this in a number of innovative ways.

Marlene thought up a catchy company name, designed a company logo and purchased a white delivery van. The white van promoted an idea of cleanliness. Marlene had some menus printed and filled baskets with freshly baked and filled baguettes and soft drinks. 'I dressed up in typical French attire and *La Baguette Du Jour* was born.'

Marlene's 'corporate image' and professional approach worked. She built a reputation for being reliable and providing high-quality products. Within twelve months Marlene had four vans and had set up an operating base on the Park employing six people and was contemplating her first retail outlet.

After the first year van sales generated weekly sales of £2500 and realised an annual net profit of about £25 000.

'My next step was to set up a take-way and patisserie in the city centre. We had capital costs of £40 000 funded by a business loan from

Midland Bank. We put a great deal of work into our business plan and developed the shop within the budgets set by the bank. Annual turnover is now running at over £350 000,' says Marlene.

Marlene's business was born from a simple idea but she has turned it into a booming success, winning small business awards and gaining respect from those who work for her.

Marlene sets a great deal of store by staff training. She also has some sound advice for other small-business operators. 'Do not lose sight of your original idea and always keep an eye on your profit margin and expenditure,' she says. 'And expand your business at a pace you are able to cope with, do thorough research and listen to customer feedback.'

✓✓✓ *Paper power*

A desire for a better quality of life, in the peace and quiet of the country, and the knowledge that more people were working from home, were inspiration for a home business set up by Andrew James and his partner, Sophie Chalmers.

In 1991 Andrew lost his job as a marketing manager and Sophie's contract as a television researcher ended. It was then that the couple decided to try doing their own thing and taking control of their lives. The pair had a flair for writing and helping others. They also realised there were thousands of people around the UK working from home and setting up their own home businesses. So they decided to set up a subscription magazine which offered support and advice for professionals working from home.

'We decided to call it *Home Run*. To get it started we used £8000 of our own savings,' says Andrew. 'In July 1992 we sent out mailshots to 15 000 potential clients. It was funded by our savings. But only 50 people took subscriptions,' says Sophie. 'We should have written the £8000 off and returned the cheques but we were too stupid. We sent out the newsletter and had two very tough years, haemorrhaging money like mad.'

By then the business was on the brink of collapse and the couple had used £22 000 of their savings. They had nothing left to pay the mortgage.

'Then an article about our magazine appeared in the *Daily Telegraph*. The renewed interest prompted more subscriptions and we started to turn a profit,' explains Andrew.

The couple then decided it was time for a quieter life. They purchased a home and old mill in Wales. 'Here we put together and dispatch our magazine to 2000 subscribers, ten times a year.'

Andrew is in charge of the technical side and Sophie, with her journalistic ability, writes it. 'We work as a team. I do the first run of the magazine and Andrew pulls together what I write,' explains Sophie. 'Our business is also a good example of how a mail-oriented business can be run from anywhere, in this case Chepstow. In a similar way we have also found the Internet extremely useful for communications between authors, printers and us. If you are a small business you should consider using the "net" if it suits your type of business,' says Andrew. 'Ours is the perfect way to run a business and have a family.'

And the couple have some tips for other home workers. Sophie says to take it step by step and to accept the bad times with the good ones. Andrew suggests that if you are a couple setting up a business together you must share the same vision. It won't work if one partner expects different things from the other.

The couple also suggest that you need to find a dedicated space in your home such as, in their case, a mill on their property to run the business. This is important not only for tax efficiency but so you can 'go to' work and 'leave' work, allowing you to separate home life from business life.

✓✓✓ *From garden shed to export glory*

A love of antique Lloyd Loom furniture has proven to be a huge money spinner for Lincolnshire's David Breese.

David used to be an antiques dealer and his clients often asked for Lloyd Loom chairs. These are chairs which were favourites of the likes of Marilyn Monroe and Sir Laurence Olivier. They look like wicker furniture but a special method of weaving and the use of paper woven around steel rods makes them withstand the damp and last for ever. It was customer interest in these antique chairs that inspired David to find out exactly how they were made.

'With some knowledge of furniture manufacturing, but with no one willing to give up the secrets of how this furniture was made, I decided to take an antique chair apart. It took four hours and I discovered how the paper and steel combination gave the chair its wicker look but increased durability,' says David.

The one problem for David, though, was just how to make the elusive weave of the chair. 'Only a few people world-wide knew and those craftspeople were loathe to give up their secret because of fear of competition.' But David was determined. He went to Ireland and within three weeks found three old looms and purchased them for £750. 'The trouble was I didn't have the faintest idea how to use them!'

So after some research David tracked down a professor at the Textile Department of Huddersfield University. He persuaded him to spend the weekend showing him how to work the looms. Then in 1987, using the machinery handbook and a great deal of trial and error, David produced a prototype chair in his garden shed.

David called his business *Lloyd Loom of Spalding* and by late 1987, using limited capital, he had rented a small unit and was producing six chairs a week. These first chairs were snapped up by a Dutch collector. From there word spread and soon David was getting phone calls from all over the world.

He uses the unique method of weaving paper around wire and fixing it onto top quality beechwood frames. Unlike wicker chairs, Lloyd Loom of Spalding chairs and furniture don't split, crack or splinter.

As business grew so did David's reputation. He used profits to expand the business and extend the product line, now producing a complete range of furniture for every room in the house. The latest designs include new contemporary furniture and accessories, in conjunction with renowned designer Geoff Hollington.

In 1995 his company won the Queen's Award for Export Achievement, with David selling to Europe, the Middle East and Asia. He has even produced chairs for the Royal Box at the All England Tennis Club Wimbledon. 'Providing chairs for the Royal Box was a significant step for the company, in that although our furniture is very competitively priced, it is high quality and is appreciated as such.'

David's success is evidence that a business idea can be turned into business reality with perseverance and research. Without David's persistence in finding out how to make the original chair and tracking down some old looms, his business would never have taken off.

Taking the business from garden shed to export glory has been tough but with the business expanding at such a remarkable rate David hasn't forgotten where he started. 'An important part of running a business is hands-on experience,' says David. And true to form David is more likely to be found on the factory floor than in the office, making sure Lloyd Loom of Spalding's quality is never surpassed.

✓✓✓ Snood and pom power

Forty-eight-year-old Maidstone dog-lover Chris Vinings has turned her passion for poodles into a unique money-making scheme.

A number of years ago Chris was showing her poodle at an open-air show, and it rained. Other poodle owners carried their dogs on their shoulders so that the clipped fur around the poodles' feet did not get wet or dirty. Chris couldn't carry her dog, and this gave her the inspiration to design special fabric protectors to stop the rounded fur on her poodle's legs getting dirty. 'I designed a tube of fabric with elastic at both ends. It slipped over the poodle's feet and covered the poms. That is what the clipped fur is called so I called the covers "poms",' says Chris.

She then started using poms at shows: other dog owners asked where she bought them. The former dressmaker admitted she made them herself and other breeders immediately put in orders. Chris started selling sets of four for £3.50.

Chris also designed snoods for her dog. 'It is an unusual name but it is a large tube of fabric with elastic at both ends and elastic ruching in the middle. It covers the poodle's head and protects the head fur and ears, allowing the dog to eat without getting its fur dirty before the show.'

Again breeders loved her designs and Chris sells her snoods for about £2.50 each. She also supplies pet stores such as Petcetera and sells by mail order to people who go to dog shows.

'It's a fun way to make a bit of extra cash and because I love poodles I have been able to create a niche market for my creations,' explains Chris.

✓✓✓ The business of bears

Izzy Shaw, at 39 years old, is proof that a passion for life can ensure business success. Izzy was battling lymph cancer when she was made redundant from her job as the coordinator for volunteer workers in the community. Undeterred, Izzy decided to take on the business world.

'I was having treatment for my cancer and knew finding work to fit my schedule would be tough. Then one day I visited a friend's bear store. They showed me a battered old teddy and I said I could repair it,' explains Izzy. She took the bear home and performed a miracle, breathing 'new life' into the old teddy.

The store's owners were so impressed they asked her to do regular repair work on bears brought in by loving owners. 'I could fit the repairs around my treatments and still earn money.'

But Izzy was unstoppable and soon realised she could design and make her own bears. She made a few samples: bears with character faces, bears with the names of children on their outfits and bears designed to celebrate births and birthdays. 'The named bears and the ones for special occasions are made on commission. I made bears originally because I was not impressed with the designs available, and the generally poor workmanship.'

Again Izzy showed the owners of the local teddy bear store, and they were impressed. 'They asked me to do a series of shop exclusives for them. I was thrilled,' says Izzy.

It was then Izzy realised this hobby was becoming a real business, so she thought up a business name, calling her bears *Izzy's Cubs*. Then she decided not to limit her designs to one store.

'I did extensive research to find out where to advertise. I narrowed it down to one teddy bear "bible", *The Teddy Bear Guide*. I contacted everyone in the Yorkshire area who dealt in teddies and sent them samples of my designs and repair work. I also took stalls at Teddy Bear Fairs.'

Izzy says the cold canvassing of stores was unnerving, but the worst was setting up stalls at fairs. 'I felt if people rejected my bears they were rejecting me, as I put so much into making them and I felt the bears were like my own children.'

But the punters loved her bears and now Izzy gets bears to repair from all over the world. Izzy now only makes one-off designs, never repeating a bear, to ensure recipients get originals with character and class.

Izzy has some tips for others who want to take on the business world. She recommends you do as much research as possible, talk to people in the trade and really listen to their advice and act on it. Izzy recommends you start small and never get behind in orders, as that will mean you risk losing your 'street cred'. A good business reputation is vital.

'There is no shame in staying small. I have decided to remain relatively small because I could never provide bears to my current quality in large numbers – after all an Izzy Cub must be special.'

✓✓✓ *Baby sling business*

A desire to keep her baby close was quite literally the inspiration behind mother of eight, Sally Wilkins' business.

When Sally had her first three children in the 1970s she was living in the south of England. When she tried to hunt down a baby sling, the few she found on the market had to be adapted so they felt comfortable and were usable. 'In true British fashion I tolerated the discomfort because I really wanted to use the slings to keep my baby close to me,' says Sally.

But then, as the children grew and Sally had another baby, she got to thinking she could design a sling of her own which would really suit mothers and babies. 'We were living in the Midlands when our fourth child, Matthew, was born, by which time I knew exactly what I needed,' explains Sally.

Sally is not a competitive person. When she designed her first baby sling all she had in mind was creating a way of keeping her baby close. 'I believe this bond strengthens the relationship between parents and babies. I knew what I wanted. It was a sling that would allow me to carry him on my front in the early months and then, as he got older and heavier, on my back. It was a sling that worked like the original shawl method of carrying a child, providing the baby with support under the thighs and bottom, and allowing the user's hands to be free.'

Sally realised the essential feature necessary to make the sling a success was comfort. Some slings used buckles that rode up the parent's back, causing discomfort, while others didn't provide enough support for the baby. So Sally developed her own sling to carry Matthew around, first drawing up a design and then sewing it together. 'Friends who saw me using the sling were impressed.'

The following summer Sally was making slings for friends from her kitchen table, and at the same time was able to be at home with her children. Then Sally took the initiative and sent a sample of her sling to the National Childbirth Trust's Technical Committee. The response was encouraging. Her inspiration was to help encourage other parents to use a sling and enjoy a close relationship with their children.

Sally then decided to send a sling to the Design Council in London and again perseverance paid off. She was awarded the coveted black and white triangle symbol for good design. By this stage Sally was calling her design a *Wilkinet*.

Sally also benefited from free publicity. Word of mouth led to baby magazines mentioning her well-designed Wilkinet. The magazines included the Wilkinet in their sling tests and Sally's product always scored well. 'It really was a case of mother knows best when it comes to designing slings,' says Sally.

Parents wrote to her praising the sling's good design and the closeness to their children it gave them. Further down the track BBC Radio's *Women's Hour* discussed the Wilkinet which was then recommended to parents.

Sally now lives in Wales and produces about 200 baby carriers a week. Wilkinets are so well made and durable that they get passed around by friends. 'We get about 30 requests each week for instructions from parents who have purchased the Wilkinet second-hand or had it handed down to them. It is reassuring to know your product is well used and loved.'

She considers it is important to target her market. She advertises in baby magazines and is included in the NCT Annual Maternity Catalogue. In the early days she also sent samples to baby experts and organisations, and from these people came reassurance, encouragement and support to press ahead with marketing the product. Word of mouth from happy parents is also important and Sally herself is a great spokesperson for her business. Her last five children are all Wilkinet babies and with eight children Sally knows what she is talking about.

'I have to admit that back in 1982, when I was making and dispatching the slings from the kitchen table, I didn't think we would soon be supplying thousands of Wilkinets to parents each year in the UK and a dozen other countries.'

In a way Sally became a business woman by accident. Her main aim was to design a good-quality sling she could use for her children. It is from these small beginnings that a healthy and steady income has grown. It's an income that means she can be a mother and a small-business person.

Sally suggests other small-business people should find an idea they really believe in and are passionate about. 'You should find ways of sharing your concept with others. If they feel the same way about your product and its benefits they, too, can spread the word.'

✓✓✓ *Cashing in on cards*

Setting up a small business does not necessarily have to be a full-time concern, as is proven by 19-year-old Rosanna Moore of Edinburgh. She's turned her hand to card-making and is cashing in, making some extra money for herself.

Two years ago Rosanna decided to save money and make her cards more personal by making her own. Her friends and family were so impressed they suggested she make some to sell. Rosanna decided to set up her business on a very small-scale basis. She spent money on raw materials and made some samples. She sold to friends and the local business community, taking orders and tailoring the cards specifically to customer needs.

'It was a good little earner and I could make the cards whenever I had time. I didn't want the business to be a big earner, as I was also looking for a full-time job. What it did allow me to do was earn some extra spending money and learn about what setting up a business really entails,' says Rosanna.

Rosanna made her small business a reality by talking to card-making experts and business chiefs to learn what she needed to know. She found her customers mainly by word of mouth and didn't have to use much set-up capital because of the low cost of materials.

'The hardest part of getting the business going was motivating myself,' explains Rosanna. 'As I worked from home I found I was easily distracted by phone calls and friends dropping in. My mind often wandered to irrelevant things. This mind-wandering meant it took longer than expected to make the cards. I had to become very focused.'

Rosanna enjoys being her own boss on a part-time basis and suggests other potential small-business operators should not expect too much out of the business in the beginning.

'Go with the flow – if the business works then great. If it doesn't, don't be discouraged. Try another approach or try another business concept. The most important thing is to make sure your business interests you.'

✓✓✓ *Tackling the fishing business*

A love of fishing, a desire to get off unemployment benefits and the Prince's Youth Business Trust were the inspiration for a second-hand fishing tackle business which is now booming for one Lincoln couple.

A few years ago Mark Marsland found himself unemployed and receiving state benefits. His partner Adele had a Diploma in Business but was pregnant with the couple's first child and finding it hard to get work. Mark was an avid fisherman but a lack of money meant that buying new tackle and upgrading rods and reels was impossible.

'Mark and his friends tried their best to overcome the problem by swapping gear but it didn't provide much relief for the fishing fanatics,' says Adele.

Then one day Mark and Adele read that fishing was Britain's number one participating hobby, with over three million anglers involved. The survey also found that a large number of the anglers were from industrial cities and mining towns. With many of the mines now closed, a great deal of people loved fishing but could not afford the tackle.

'Mark is someone who was brought up to believe you do not get rich working for other people. So we sat down and did some thinking.' The couple came up with a solution. They decided to offer a service where second-hand tackle could be bought or exchanged. Mark had the fishing knowledge and Adele had the business qualifications through her studies. But the couple were facing a crisis themselves. There was little money coming in, the baby was due soon and the rent on the one-bedroom flat was a problem.

However, undeterred and determined to be their own bosses, the couple ploughed on. First they took advantage of a 'free ad' scheme run by their local newspaper. 'We asked people if they had second-hand tackle they wanted to sell. Then in the second advertisement we were selling second-hand tackle. We expected a few calls but were overwhelmed by the number of phone calls. We had one caller who had tackle to sell, and we made our first purchase for £40. The first calls took almost every penny we had. It was a gamble. Mark priced the tackle, using a national fishing magazine, and then we went to a car boot sale,' says Adele.

'It worked,' explains Mark. 'It cost us about £10 for the table and the cost of taking part in the boot sale, and we sold our tackle and made £80. It was great.'

The next day the couple went to the Sunday market. 'The stand cost £25. We ended up making £120 and sold nearly all the stock,' explained Mark.

At this point the couple knew they were on to something. They drew up a business plan but raising capital was hard. 'We lived in a rented flat, had an £800 car, were both unemployed and had a new baby.' Then the couple heard about the Prince's Youth Business Trust, which was set up by HRH Prince of Wales in 1986 to help young people, who could not get finance through normal channels, to set up businesses.

The Trust, however, took a great deal of convincing. The couple had to devise a thorough business and marketing plan and convince the Trust that their business made sound economic sense. 'The Trust listened and offered us a loan of £500 and a grant of £1500.' The Trust also allocated the couple a business adviser. Slowly the business grew and after three years the couple now have a shop, a mail-order client base and projected annual turnover of £160 000. The couple have also won awards for their business and even met Prince Charles who is the Trust's patron and a keen fisherman. The couple also help encourage other young business people.

Their advice – listen to others and extract as much free information from experts as possible. 'Don't be influenced in decisions by family and friends, and plough every piece of profit into your business,' says Mark. 'In the first few years the business needs all the support it can get – buying flash cars and going on holidays is a recipe for disaster. Work hard at growing your business and developing your skills.'

Adele also suggests you must have a determination and willingness to work long and hard hours. 'Also, if you think you qualify, contact the Prince's Youth Business Trust. They can provide you with expert help and advice. They certainly gave us the chance we needed.'

2
WHAT YOU NEED TO KNOW

In this chapter, we cover:

- some useful terms that will be used in this book and in business
- a few dos and don'ts
- how to set up an office in your home
- tips for success in business
- some useful addresses in the UK and Europe
- helpful government programmes
- possible sources of financial assistance
- legal aspects.

Setting up a business

When you first consider setting up a business you may be over-whelmed with everything that is involved – budgeting, finances, marketing advertising, product development and so on. To get you started here are some useful business terms that I shall be using all the way through this book.

Useful terms

Advertising Advertising can take various forms, such as printed advertisements and fliers. It tells people about your service or product – people can't buy unless they know you are selling.

Budget   This is the way you plan to allocate the money, on a weekly, monthly or yearly basis, to run your business.

Business cards   These small cards are an excellent way to promote your business and to establish credibility.

Business names   Business names need to be registered; the name you use must not already be registered by another business – if it is, you must choose another one.

Business plan   An overview of your business and product or service, which also includes industry, marketing and financial information. Essential for obtaining financing, venture capital or investors.

Capital   The funds and equipment used for production.

Cash flow   The movement of money into and out of a business, resulting from ongoing operations and any other sources and uses of funds.

Competition   Other businesses that offer products or services similar to yours.

Cost   The monetary value of time, materials and anything else required to produce goods or perform a service.

Dial a service   A modern trend: you phone for a service and it comes to your door.

Expense   Money spent for the business, incidental to production, such as advertising, stationery and legal fees.

Feedback   What your customers tell you about your product or service. Use it to improve your product or service.

Flier   A multi-purpose promotion tool that can be used for letter-box drops, leafleting and inclusion with products you sell. It tells people about your service and your products.

Gimmick   An unusual idea or method to attract attention and make your business stand out.

Income   The net amount of money you earn from selling your product or providing a service, after deduction of all costs and expenses. You may be eligible to pay tax, if your income exceeds a certain amount. Check with the Inland Revenue if you are in doubt.

Inventory   The amount of the product you have in stock.

Loans   Small-business loans provide capital for large items. You must include the costs of loan repayments in your budget.

Market   The people who use your service or buy your product. You must know your customers in order to target them in your advertising and promotions.

Mobile phone and pager   Communication devices that make it easy for your customers to reach you.

Press release   A way of letting the media know that your business is possibly news-worthy.

Pricing   Determining the fee for your service or product. Pricing covers costs and includes a profit margin.

Product   The goods you produce for sale.

Profit   The amount of revenue in excess of your costs and pre-tax expenses.

Risk   The possibility of incurring a loss.

Sales (or revenue)   The money you receive in exchange for goods or services provided.

Service   Work done (usually for payment) to meet a need.

Tax   A contribution levied by the government on individuals, property or businesses. (*See* Tax section.)

Trend   A general tendency or direction influencing what consumers want to buy.

Dos and don'ts

Once you have decided to set up a small business it is important to clarify the dos and don'ts of the business world. For example making a profit may seem like a very basic concept but many small business operators fail to do this. They often under-price their service or product because they want to attract customers; then in the long term their business fails.

Read through this list of dos and don'ts and identify how each one will affect your proposed small business.

Do

Make a profit

The whole idea of being in business is to make a profit. It may sound obvious but, believe me, many business people out there don't realise they aren't making any money. Make sure you work out all the costs involved in your product or service, and always allow for a reasonable profit margin.

Research your market

Know who you want to target, and design your product or service with that group in mind. Your advertising and selling efforts will be much more effective if you are focused.

Watch trends

If your business is in any way affected by trends, try to work out how it can still be popular one year, two years or five years from now. Your product or service may have to evolve, changing with client demands. You may also have to add extra services or increase your product range to maintain your success. Keep abreast of trends: read magazines and trade journals relevant to your business, and watch the competition.

Contact experts and professional organisations for advice

They can help you with financial, legal and general business issues. They may also provide courses which will enhance your business skills.

Stick to your budget

Make a budget for your business and stick to it. You must plan your finances carefully.

Get feedback from customers

Constantly ask clients for feedback. Get their opinions and ask them how you can make your product or service better.

Don't

Don't throw good money after bad

Many small-business people think that throwing money at a problem will fix it. Money, however, is not always the answer. If people are not buying, ask them why. If you want to attract more customers, work out how to reach your target demographic group, instead of simply buying a bigger, more colourful advertisement. Research your problem and discuss it with the experts before investing in an expensive course of action.

Don't over-extend

Do not over-commit yourself financially or promise customers more than you can actually provide. Growing too quickly or over-extending your resources can be detrimental to your business.

Don't listen to people who merely *claim* to be experts

Make sure the accountants, lawyers, financial advisers and other experts you use are reputable, accredited and experienced in their fields. The advice they give can make the difference between success and failure.

Don't be hasty when considering a loan

If you decide to take out a small-business loan, choose a reputable bank or lending society. Shop around to get the best deal and the most competitive rates. Do not feel obliged to accept the first loan offered. Beware of loan sharks and those without proper credentials.

Don't expect to become a millionaire overnight

Making money takes time and effort. If you are not prepared to work hard and put in long hours, then you should go back to your nine-to-five job.

——— Setting up a home office ———

Most of the small business ideas included in this book can be done from home. If you are planning to work from home, it is important that you set aside a space in your house or flat for your business office. A study, a corner of the bedroom or living room will do. This will become your business headquarters; when you use this space you forget about the worries of the home and direct all your attention to your business.

A home office will need a number of things.

A computer, a printer and a desk   Many homes now have computers and they can be used for keeping business records, designing fliers and product planning. If you don't have a computer perhaps you might consider renting one or buying second-hand. Before you do this, visit a number of dealers and ask their advice. Tell them exactly what you want to use the computer for and how much you can afford to spend.

Filing cabinet
You can pick up a second-hand filing cabinet or perhaps purchase an expanding cardboard file for around £5–10. This will keep all your receipts and documentation together.

Phone or mobile phone
Consider getting a separate phone line for your business, or purchasing a mobile phone. This allows you to be easily accessible and allows prospective clients to contact you when they need to.

Docket book and diary
These should be kept somewhere that is easily accessible. The diary allows you to plan the development of your small business and keep track of appointments and meetings. The docket book allows you to keep track of sales and purchases and is important for tax.

Office supplies
These include pens, pencils, paper and staples. They don't have to be fancy, merely practical; and remember when setting up your first business, try to keep costs low.

The most important aspect of a home office is to define it as your personal business space. It is not a place for children to play or for homework to be done. This is an important aspect of your business and you need to treat it as you would if it were an office in the city.

Business tips

Here are some important tips you should remember when setting up a small business.

Plan for the future

Always be thinking ahead. Put aside money for expanding your operations, and also for emergencies and lean times. If you talk to successful small-business entrepreneurs, they will tell you they sell today but live for the next month, the next year or the next decade. They are always thinking about improving and expanding their business.

Know when to stop

The reality of running a small business is that many do fail. It may be for any one of a number of reasons, such as cash-flow problems, poor timing or heavy competition. You must be prepared for failure if it does happen. Know when to say 'enough is enough' and then get out. Don't simply get another loan from the bank and bury yourself in debt – close down the business and take a break. Then, when you feel confident and financially secure, try again with a different idea.

Have fun

You've decided to work for yourself because it was your dream – make sure you enjoy that dream.

UK and European business contacts

In the previous pages I have suggested you contact small business groups and government departments for information, when setting up your business. But just how do you wade through the plethora of listings in the phone book? Here are some contact addresses that you will probably find useful.

Federation of Small Businesses

Head Office
32 St Anne's Road West
Lytham St Annes
Lancashire FY8 1NY
☎ 01253 720911

London Office
2 Catherine Place
Westminster
London SW1E 6HF
☎ 0171 233 7900

The Federation of Small Businesses is a non-profit making organisation and is the major organisation in the UK and Europe representing the interests of the self-employed and people who direct small business in the UK. It provides members with access to telephone help lines, expert advice on legal, business and personal matters, as well as taxation and insurance matters.

British Franchising Association

Thames View
Newtown Road
Henley on Thames RG9 1HG
☎ 01491 578 049

Banking Ombudsman

70 Grays Inn Road
London WC1X 8NB
☎ 0171 404 9944

**Building Societies
 Ombudsman Scheme**
Millbank Tower
Millbank
London SW1P 4XS

National Debtline
☎ 0121 359 8501

Prince's Youth Business Trust
18 Park Square
London NW1 4LH
☎ 0171 543 1234

**The Chambers of Commerce
 of Ireland**
22 Merrion Square
Dublin
Ireland

The Trademarks Registry
25 Southampton Buildings
Chancery Lane
Holborn
London WC2A 1AY
☎ 0171 438 4700

Welsh Development Agency
Head Office
Principality House
The Friary
Cardiff

**Scottish Office Information
 Directorate**
New St Andrews House
Edinburgh
EH1 3TD

Office of Fair Trading
Field House
15–25 Bream's Buildings
London EC4A 1PR
☎ 0171 242 2858

Patent Office
Head Office
Concept House
Cardiff Road
Newport
South Wales NP9 1RH

Scottish Enterprise
120 Bothwell Street
Glasgow G2 7JP

**Association of British
 Chambers of Commerce**
9 Tufton Street
London SW1P 3QB
☎ 0171 565 2000

Home Run
(Magazine for small-business
operators working at home)
Cribau Mill
Llanvair Discoed
Chepstow NP6 6RD
☎ 01291 641 222

**Northern Ireland
 Information Service**
Stormont Castle
Belfast BT4 3ST

Welsh Office
Cathays Park
Cardiff CF1 3NQ

Commonwealth Development Corporation
1 Bessborough Gardens
London SW1P 2JQ

The Institute of Trade Mark Agents
4th Floor
Canterbury House
2–6 Sydenham Road
Croydon CR0 9XE

European Commission
Jean Monnet House
8 Storey's Gate
London SW1P 3AT
☎ 0171 973 1992

Companies Registration Office
Companies House
Crown Way
Cardiff CF4 3UZ

Confederation Of British Industry
Centrepoint
103 New Oxford Street
London WC1A 1DU

Here are some useful addresses in European countries. If you want to set up a small business in these countries, or you want to do business in these countries, start by contacting their national chamber of commerce and asking for useful addresses and business information.

Austria
Wirtschaftskammer Osterreich
Weidner Hauptstr 63
1040 Wien

Belgium
Chambers of Commerce
Avenue Louise 500
B1050 Brussels

Bulgaria
Bulgarian Chamber of Commerce
and Industry
11A Sveorna St
Sofia 1000

Cyprus
Cyprus CCI
PO Box 1455
Nicosia 1509

Czech Republic
The Economic Chamber of the
Czech Republic
Ma Vacslyna 30
Praha 10
Scrasnaci

Denmark
Danish Chamber of Commerce
Borsen
Copenhagen K 1271

Finland
Central Chamber of Commerce
PO Box 1000
00101 Helsinki

France
Assemblee des Chambres
    Francaises de Commerce
    et d'Industrie (ACFCI)
BP 448-16
Paris 75116

Germany
Deutscher Industrie und Handelstag
PS 1446
5300 Bonn

Greece
Union of Hellenic Chambers
    of Commerce
Akadimias 7/9
Athens 10671

Hungary
Hungarian Chamber of Commerce
    and Industry
1005 Budapest
Kossuth Lajos ter 6–8

Iceland
Iceland Chamber
    of Commerce
Vus Verslunarinnar Kringlan 7
Reykjvik 103

Israel
Federation of Israeli
    Chambers of Commerce
PO Box 2007
Tel Aviv

Italy
Unione Italiana della CCIAA
Piazza Sallustio 21
Rome 00187

Luxembourg
Chambre de Commerce du
    Grand Duché de Luxembourg
7 Rue Alcide de Gasperi
Luxembourg 1051

Malta
The Malta Chamber of Commerce
Exchange Building
Republic Street
Valletta

The Netherlands
Vereniging van Kamers
    van Koophandel en Fabrieken
    in Nederland
PO Box 265
3440 AG Woerden

Poland
Polish Chamber of Commerce
Ul. Trebacka 4
00074 Warszawa

Portugal
Associacao Comercial de Lisboa
CCI Portuguesa
89 Rua Portas de Santo Antao
1150 Lisboa

Romania
CCI of Romania
22 N. Balescu Boulevard
Bucharest 79502

Slovakia
Slovak Chamber of Commerce
   and Industry
Gorkeho Str 9
Bratislava 81603

Spain
Official Chamber of Commerce
Huertas No. 13
Madrid

Switzerland
Schweizerischer Handels
   und Industrieverein
Mainaustrasse 49
8034 Zurich

Slovenia
Chamber of Economy
Slovenska Cesta 4
Ljubljana 1504

Sweden
Stockholm Chamber of Commerce
Box 16050
SE–103 21
Stockholm

Turkey
Union of CCI
Ataturk Bulvari 149
Ankara

— UK Government help programmes —

If you are considering setting up a small business you should contact the Federation of Small Businesses. The address is listed above.

Business Link

If your business is in the UK you should also contact Business Link in your town or capital city. Business Link is a network of offices that provides a single point of access for all key local business support agencies.

If you meet their selection criteria, they can provide new business operators with advice and support to establish a new venture. You will receive expert counselling and help, from the planning stage right through to the launch of your business. Once the business is established, Business Link can provide you with quarterly reviews to make sure everything is running smoothly. Business Link can also help you identify financing options to ensure you get the best possible start to your business life.

The address and telephone number of Business Link in your local area is in the phone book or you could try this address.

Business Link

London City Partners
78 Great Eastern Street
London EC2A 3JL
☎ 0171 324 2700

Department of Trade and Industry

The Department of Trade and Industry (DTI) produces a series of booklets for small businesses. You can contact the local office of the DTI by looking in your phone book or by ringing 0114 259 7535. You can also write, to receive small business publications.

Publications Section (Department of Trade and Industry)
Level 2
St Mary's House
c/o Moorfoot
Sheffield
S1 4PQ

Inland Revenue

The Inland Revenue also produces a series of booklets for small-business operators. These booklets outline your tax requirements and responsibilities, who you need to notify if you are setting up a small business, and what your national insurance and VAT requirements are.

Contact the Inland Revenue office in your city or town and ask for a copy of their 'Starting Your Own Business' brochure and their 'Self Assessment – A Guide for the Self-employed' pamphlet. Better still, visit your local office and sit down with a tax office representative and ask them to talk you through how you will pay tax if you are a small business operator.

Job Centre

Visit your local Job Centre and ask them if they have any leaflets on setting up a small business.

Remember government offices are a valuable resource and if you can cut through the red tape by being direct with your questions you can do some valuable research this way.

— Where to find financial assistance —

When setting up your business you may find a number of schemes useful. If you qualify for help, the following schemes can provide you with funds to cover set-up costs.

While most of the business ideas in this book require limited capital of £50–100 to set up, you may in time want to expand. That is when you may have to seek extra financial help.

Short-term overdrafts

A bank or building society may consider letting you have a short-term overdraft facility. It is quite simple and normally quick to organise but you should remember that the bank may demand immediate repayment of the money or you may have to offer a guarantee of payment in the form of a personal asset, such as your house.

Taking on a partner

When expanding you may like to take on a partner, who will bring with them extra funds. However, you must make sure that legal agreements governing your rights and those of your partner, and their share of profit, are drawn up.

Long-term loans

Banks and building societies offer a range of long-term loans with varying interest rates. To take advantage of these loans you must present your bank manager with a detailed business plan and cash-flow projection.

Legal requirements

When you set up your own business you must be aware of the legal requirements your business must meet. Here is a list of things you will need to do.

- Define your business organisation. In the UK there are two legal forms of business groups – unincorporated bodies and corporated bodies (see below).
- Inform the Inland Revenue (income tax). The tax office needs to know about the new business and the fact you have started trading. Contact your local tax office and ask them for a form 41G. This requires you to fill out basic details such as the business name, your business address and the date you started trading.
- Talk to Social Security. You must work out what your national insurance contributions and VAT liabilities will be (see Chapter 3).

If you start out small then you will be setting up as an **unincorporated body**. That means the business is run by one person, known as a **sole trader**, or a group of people, known as a **partnership**, trading for a common purpose. Most of the businesses in this book are the type to be set up by a sole trader. You must therefore be aware of laws relating to the sale of goods, consumer protection and employment protection.

Contact your local Department of Trade and Industry and ask them for information about the following laws – remember it will pay to be informed.

- Sale of Goods Act 1979
- The Supply of Goods and Services Act 1982
- The Consumer Protection Act 1987
- The Trade Descriptions Act 1972.

And if you employ someone even on a casual or part-time basis, get to know the Employment Protection Act 1978.

In the UK, there is a free advisory service, the **Citizens' Advice Bureau**, that will be able to give you basic information about the legal aspects, and they will also be able to advise where to get further information, if they cannot provide it. The bureaux are often based in or near public libraries, and are listed in the phone book. They make an excellent starting-off point, if you really don't know who to turn to for advice.

3

BUSINESS MATTERS

Once you have an idea for your own business, there are some things you need to sort out. You will need to know about:

- business plans
- handling cash flow
- how to set prices and what profit to expect
- how to identify the market for your business
- what you will be liable to pay in the way of taxes and national insurance.

A business plan

Every business, no matter how small, needs a business plan. It will help you form a clear picture of your financial situation now and in the future, and it will be necessary if you are seeking financial assistance or backing, or wish to attract investors.

Your business plan may include the following components:

- a description of your product or service
- an overview of your business operations and technology
- an industry overview and competitive analysis
- an overview of the market and trends
- a comprehensive marketing plan
- pro forma financial statements, cash flow statements, growth projections and other financial information

- identification of opportunities and challenges
- details of management and staffing
- a timetable for the business
- any other relevant issues, documentation and appendices.

Your business plan must also detail the amount of capital you have available for set-up and projected costs, as well as projected sales. This allows you to work out whether you have enough money, and ensure that you are not going to be under-capitalised. Remember poor financial planning is the main reason small businesses fail. A small-business plan will help you remain focused and goal-oriented, and that is half the battle.

No matter what type of business you are setting up, I recommend that you either do a course in running a small business, or contact the Federation of Small Businesses or your nearest Business Link scheme for help with a business plan. You could also try your local bank or building society, especially if you require some form of overdraft to help set up your business.

If you have an accountant who manages your tax affairs talk to their office, and if you have legal concerns contact a lawyer. Never ever adopt the 'It'll be OK' attitude. Careful planning will pay off in the long run.

Cash flow

Cash flow is the movement of money in and out of a business, as a result of ongoing operations and any other sources and uses of funds. Cash-flow problems occur when there is a net outflow (more going out than coming in) and, hence, insufficient funds to cover day-to-day operations. Cash-flow problems are a major difficulty for new businesses and can often be the factor that makes the business fail.

Even though you may have a brilliant business idea, a good product or service and a lucrative market, you may still run short of funds. For instance, you may have bills to pay now, while your customers aren't due to pay you for another 30 days. Or, perhaps, too many of your clients are falling behind in their payments. If you have clients who take goods or services on account, be sure to check their credit ratings as part of the approval process. In general, you should monitor your cash flow carefully to ensure the smooth operation of your business.

Example

Tom's London Window Washing

1 January 1998

Capital	£200
Equipment purchase	£50
Newspaper advertisements	£50
Fliers	£30
Mobile phone	£50

Estimated sales

January

Incoming

3 customers a week at £30 a time	£360

Outgoing

Transport costs	£40
Replenish cleaning fluids	£10

February

Incoming

5 customers a week at £30 a time	£600

Outgoing

Transport costs	£40
Replenish cleaning fluids	£10
Extra newspaper advertisements	£30
Extra fliers	£30

March

Incoming

7 customers a week at £30 a time	£840

Outgoing

Transport costs	£40
Replenish fluids	£10
Extra advertisements	£30
Extra fliers	£30

These projections show Tom's market is growing and out of his income each month he can expect costs to total around £110.

From the remaining income Tom must pay his income tax and national insurance and then enjoy his profits. The estimates of cash flow also reveal Tom will be able to recoup his capital investment of £200 by the second or third month, depending on customer growth and the success of his advertising. If the customer numbers do not meet projected estimates, Tom should reassess how he is targeting his market and look at ways of improving advertising.

Pricing and profit

You must watch your margins carefully – there's no point in running a business if you don't make any money. Someone I knew who was running a business had lots of customers and orders, but wasn't making money. The reason: the product was being sold at cost because of the fear that if the price were raised, then people wouldn't buy.

This is an example of low business confidence and poor planning. I sat down with this person and explained that it was OK to include in the price the cost of labour and a reasonable profit margin. The customers were not going to leave in droves – the product was a good one and, after all, this person wasn't running a charity.

To maximise your profits, you'll want to charge as much as you can, while keeping in line with market prices. To determine market prices, take into account shop prices, newspaper and direct-mail advertising and any other sources of pricing information available to you. Check the price guidelines in this book, but keep in mind that there will be price differentials, for example, from region to region and between urban and country areas.

Compare your findings on market prices with your costs. Then work out your profit margins and prices. The price you decide on may be higher or lower than the market price, depending on your strategy and the positioning of the product. For example, you may decide on a lower price than the market, receiving a lower-than-average profit margin per product, but making up for the lower margin through high-volume sales. Or, you may choose to charge a premium for a high-quality product, with high profit margins per product. There are numerous possibilities.

To work out your profit margin:

take your price (P) and subtract any costs (C) involved in making the product, as well as expenses (E) allocated to the product. The difference is your profit margin (M).

$$M = P - (C + E)$$

To determine your profit margin as a percentage, divide your profit margin (M) by costs and expenses ($C + E$) and multiply by 100%.

Percentage profit margin $= \dfrac{M}{C + E} \times 100\%$

For example, if your product costs £10 to make (including expenses) and your price is £14, then your profit margin is £4. And, $4 \div 10 = 0.4$ (i.e. a 40 per cent margin).

For a service, work out your margins based on costs and price per hour or per project. Usually 25–40 per cent is a reasonable profit margin, however the percentage can vary greatly, depending on your product or service, the quantities you produce and your costs.

Test your price in the market. If people are willing to pay more, then you can increase your price and thus increase your profit margin. If your prices are higher than the market is willing to bear, you can either try to enhance the product or service to make it worth the extra money, or lower your price. If you must lower your price, you can maintain your profit margin by decreasing your costs through efficiency, or you may have to consider sacrificing some quality. You can also make up for lower margins by selling more of your product.

Sample list of costs and expenses

Here is a sample list of costs and expenses you should consider when working out your pricing and your profit margin:

- raw materials
- labour
- transport costs
- tools and equipment
- uniforms
- licence fees/permits
- advertising
- fliers
- business cards
- stationery
- office supplies
- rent (for office space; storage space)
- phone
- power
- gas
- expert fees (legal, accounting, etc.)
- bank charges.

Market identification

Having a good idea for setting up your own business is just the start. You must understand exactly who will use your service, in order to target your market and advertise to them. Here are some tips.

Profile your customer

Make a list of the types of people who would use your service. Categorise them by age, gender, social background and income: this is your **demographic** picture. Profiling your customer in this way will help you determine which magazines and newspapers best target your market.

Analyse feedback

Client feedback is essential. Ask enquirers how they heard about you: keep a tally and you'll gradually develop a picture of the best way to advertise.

Find out what your customers want

Ask clients if they are happy with the quality of service, if they have any suggestions to improve the service and if there are any other products or services they think you should be offering. You could also leave an evaluation form at the end of the job.

Remember, you are in the business of supplying what the customer wants, not what you want to supply. If you want to make sales, don't try to sell the customer what you *think* they want, sell them what they *really* want. Listen to their demands and then genuinely try to provide that.

Small-business taxes

There are many people who want to set up a small business but are put off the idea because of tax. Just thinking about receiving a tax bill frightens many, while others believe all their profit and in turn their hard work will be eaten up by the tax office.

I strongly recommend that you employ an accountant to work out your tax for you. This way you can ensure the tax form, when submitted, is done thoroughly. However, as a small-business operator you should understand what your tax commitments are and how a tax bill is determined. Here are some important facts, as they relate to the UK.

- The tax year runs from April 6 through to April 5 the following year.
- A new system of income tax was introduced for self-employed people in April 1997. It is called self-assessment and the Inland Revenue says it is a more straightforward and efficient way of working out tax. Broadly speaking, your tax assessment will be based on your business profits for the accounting year which ends in the same tax year.
- Each year in April the Inland Revenue will send you a tax return schedule. The information you provide on the schedule will help calculate your income tax and capital gains tax bill for that financial year. You can then complete the schedule yourself and send it back to the tax office where your tax due will be calculated. The form must arrive by 30 September.
- You can calculate tax due yourself, or ask an accountant to do it for you. These forms must be lodged before January 31.
- If you fail to meet these deadlines you will pay a penalty of £100.
- On the new forms you will be required to give your income figures so make sure all your records are accurate. You must also include gains, reliefs and deductions. If you work through the schedule and follow the instructions you should be able to determine the amount of tax you have to pay.
- The new self-assessment system now means you do not have to send in your accounts with your tax return. Instead you will be asked to include accounts information in a special section of the return. Remember you are ultimately responsible for the accuracy of these details.
- Tax deemed payable on the self-assessment form will be due by 31 January following the tax year covered by the return.
- To order leaflets about self-assessment call the special Self-Assessment Response Line ☎ 0345 16 15 14 or contact your local tax office.

- You can also call the Self-Assessment Helpline ☎ 0645 000 444. It's open Monday – Friday 5 p.m. – 10 p.m. and on Saturday and Sunday 8 a.m. – 10 p.m.

National insurance

In the UK, if you work then you are liable to pay national insurance (social security) contributions. Self-employed people are liable to pay two classes of contribution. These are the basic Class 2 contributions and Class 4 paid on profit and gains.

Class 2

These contributions are a flat-rate payment collected by the Contributions Agency. In 1996–7 the weekly rate was £6.05. For further information about paying Class 2 through direct debit write to:

Direct Debit Section
Contributions Agency
Longbenton
Newcastle upon Tyne NE98 1YX

Class 4

If you make a profit or gain over a certain level, as set by the chancellor in the annual budget, you must pay Class 4 contributions. In 1996–7 the rate was six per cent.

The lower profit level was £6860 and the upper profit level was £23 660.

For further information about national insurance contact your local Social Security Office.

You can also get advice from your local Tax Office or Tax Enquiry Centre, Monday to Friday. Or you can phone for advice on National Insurance, ☎ 0800 666 555, or in Northern Ireland, ☎ 0800 616 757.

VAT

You should also ask your accountant if you should be registered for Value Added Tax or VAT. This is a tax charged on most goods and services by suppliers of those goods and services. Whether you need to be VAT-registered depends on your turnover. Contact your local VAT Business Advice Centre for further information. The number is in the phone book. You can also call a special telephone hotline ☎ 0345 16 15 14.

Other useful addresses

If you have a complaint about the way your tax or national insurance has been handled contact:

The Adjudicator's Office
Haymarket House
28 Haymarket
London SW1Y 4SP
☎ 0171 930 2292

You can also ask a Member of Parliament to refer your complaint to the Ombudsman. You can get further information by writing to:

The Parliamentary Commissioner for Administration
Church House
Great Smith Street
London SW1P 3BW

Or, if you are in Northern Ireland:

The Parliamentary Ombudsman and Commissioner for Complaints
Progressive House
33 Wellington Place
Belfast
BT1 6GD

4

MARKET RESEARCH AND ADVERTISING

Before your business can take off, you need to consider where the money will come from, where the customers will come from, how you will attract them. You must think about:

- set-up costs
- adjusting your costs to the funds you have available
- advertising
- a business image
- telling people about your business
- telling people who you are
- keeping people informed.

– The cost of starting your business –

Most of the ideas suggested in this book can be set up with small amounts of capital. However, each small business is different and, thus, will have different start-up costs. In some cases, your capital might be as small as £60 to cover the first newspaper advertisement and fliers, or it might be £5000 to buy equipment and set up shop.

Determine how much you can afford to spend on setting up your money-making scheme. Be slightly generous in your estimates of how much it will cost you. A little extra padding never hurt anyone, and it provides you with a measure of safety, should you have unforeseen costs. Once you have decided on a reasonable figure, stick to it. Do not fall into the trap of saying, 'If I spend another £100, the business will work.' You could end up spending thousands and getting nowhere.

Making the most of a limited budget

Because you are probably starting up your business with a small amount of capital, you must be thrifty and learn to make the most of your limited budget. Again this is where planning and research come in. Once you have determined just who wants to use or buy your services, work out the best possible way to get the message to those people.

Start by making a list of the publications they will read. For example *Donnie's Dog Walking* is based in Camden Town and is available to people living in that particular area. So Donnie takes out an **advertisement** in the pet section in the local paper, puts up **posters** he made himself at local pet stores and does a **flier** drop of the neighbourhood. Donnie also targets pet owners when they are walking their dogs, so he visits the local parks and hands out **business cards** there. He puts posters up on traffic lights, in the local supermarket and visits church and social groups to tell them about his service. Donnie also targets local doctors' surgeries and is allowed to put up posters so that if someone is ill they know who to call so their pet still gets a walk.

Donnie enlists the help of family and friends when handing out fliers and gets a group of people together to make colourful posters. He also talks to dog and pet groups when they have their meetings each month.

Yes, there is a lot of foot slogging but instead of spending large sums of money Donnie only has to pay for a small advertisement in the local paper and for the cost of fliers and posters.

When trying to make the most of a limited budget think laterally and do not be afraid to ask friends to help you out.

Advertising

Advertising can take various forms, such as printed advertisements and fliers. Advertising is vital because it tells people about your service or product – people can't buy unless they know you are selling.

Print advertising

Many of the money-making ideas in this book rely on advertising in newspapers or magazines. But simply putting an advertisement in the local paper may not mean you'll be a huge success. The entry has to be interesting and catch the reader's eye. Here are my tips for making sure you get noticed.

Where to advertise

It is important to profile your customer and direct your message to the key buyers you identify. You should get copies of all the local papers, newsletters and magazines in which you're thinking of advertising. Read the articles and study the magazines: are they the types your prospective customers read? You can also ring the sales department of each of these publications and get a demographic breakdown of their readership. They'll tell you the age group, income group and gender favouring their publication. Knowing this will help you determine whether the publication reaches your target market effectively.

Remember when starting out, local papers are the best starting point rather than big nationals – and they are cheaper too.

Planning your advertising

To be a success, your advertisement must be noticed. Consider using bold type or a design to draw attention to your advertisement. At the very least, a line of stars or asterisks is a good attention grabber.

Providing information

Make sure your advertisement provides the reader with information. Include your business name, contact name, phone number, a short description of what you offer and starting prices. Remember that many people are put off if the price is not stated. You should also emphasise personal service. If you provide same-day service, highlight the fact. Draw attention to all the good features of the goods or services you are offering – without turning the advertisement into an essay!

Bargain hunting

Take advantage of special promotional offers on advertising in newspapers, such as 'two-for-the-price-of-one' opportunities or 'buy a Saturday entry and get a Monday entry free'. Talk to the sales people and ask them about deals they offer – there are discounts to be had.

Be careful when buying advertising space. Do not buy over the phone from people who make unsolicited telephone calls with spectacular offers. It is not uncommon for people to ring the unwary claiming to be from a familiar-sounding magazine and offering amazing deals, but a little checking often reveals either the magazine doesn't exist or these people do not work for it. If you suspect foul play, ask to see the advertising rep's credentials and ring the office to verify them.

Consumer feedback

Ask your clients how they found out about your service and keep a record of their answers: word-of-mouth, posters, fliers or advertisements. By doing so, you can work out the most effective form of advertising for your business.

Sample advertisements

✪✪✪ PAWS 4 THOUGHT ✪✪✪

Let Helen look after your pet while you are on holiday!
Daily feeding, walking and watering.
Grooming and home security checks.
References and police checks provided.
Call Helen any time for free quote.
☎ 0171 123 4567

✪✪✪ PAWS 4 THOUGHT ✪✪✪

THE GRASSKEEPER

No job too big or small.
Lawns mowed, gardens weeded, trees pruned and gutters cleaned.
Free quotes, senior citizen discounts.
Charges from £12 an hour.
References supplied.
If you're not happy with the job, you don't pay.
☎ John 0181 123 4567 any time.

THE GRASSKEEPER

——— Business name ———

A snappy business name will often be an excellent way of generating publicity all by itself. For example Toys R Us has seen a range of firms copy the name concept, now there are Bins 4 Us, Made 4 TV, Computers R U etc.

A catchy name is also easier for people to remember and if it stays in their mind they are more likely to contact you. So brainstorm with family and friends to come up with a great name people will not soon forget.

If you want to ensure no one else uses your business name or your logo you should register it with the Patent Office. You can write to them for further information.

Patent Office
Head Office
Concept House
Cardiff Road
Newport
South Wales
NP9 1RH

Press release

When you set up a money-making venture, free publicity is important. You can pay for newspaper advertisements and put up as many posters as you like, but a newspaper article, or coverage on a television or radio news programme, will probably reach more people and won't cost you any money. So, how do you interest hard-bitten journalists and convince them that your business is newsworthy?

A well-constructed press release with a 'news angle' is the answer. Sounds easy? Well, it can be if you use your head. Here is a guide.

- Type your press release neatly on a sheet of A4 paper. Use letter-head stationery if you have it.
- Put the press release title in bold type at the top of the page. The title must be catchy and immediately grab the reader's interest. For example, a title like 'New business caring for pets set up' is boring. The press release would be ignored and thrown in the bin. However a title like 'Pet beautician beats doggie glamour blues' has a dramatically different impact. It's catchy and encourages the journalist to read on to find out more.
- Include the date of the press release next to the title. The date is essential because releases often get mixed up and are resorted by date.
- Use the 'inverted pyramid method' for writing your release. Put the most important and interesting facts in the first paragraph, and the least important fact in the last paragraph. The body of the press release should be about seven to eight paragraphs long. There should be no more than two sentences per paragraph, and your sentences should be short, simple and concise.
- Keep the release newsy and interesting. Don't be afraid to use quotations from yourself or testimonials from satisfied customers. Quotations give the story a ring of authenticity, and are especially convincing if they are from customers. Journalists may be able to use them in their stories. If a journalist rings you to do a story, offer to put him/her in touch with clients who have used your services, to get both sides of the story. Representing both sides will make the story more newsy and objective.
- At the bottom of the page, put:
  For further information call: (*add your name and contact number*)

The journalist can easily contact you to check facts, or organise an interview or photo session.

- You should send the press release to the chief of staff, forward-planning desk or day editor of the local paper, radio and television stations.

Sample Press Release

Birmingham Girl Beats the Unemployment Diet Checking 4/3/98

A 19-year-old Birmingham woman who refused to apply for government benefits is now cashing in, making sure other people stick to their diets.

Joan Smith couldn't get a job and finally decided to create her own work. She helps people stick to their diets by making unannounced visits to check their fridge and cupboard for fatty food.

'I make lightning diet raids on my clients' homes. I check to see if they are sticking to their diet, I check the house for unhealthy, anti-diet food and I talk to my clients about how their diet is going. I provide moral support and the toughness to throw any fatty food out,' explains Joan.

Joan's idea to set up her diet checking service came after her own battle to keep the weight off failed. 'I'd just start losing it when I'd break the diet. Then it hit me, if I had someone to check on my diet each day or every second day, life would be a lot easier and I'd be a lot skinnier,' says Joan.

Betty Dobbs, a 25-year-old mother of two, is one satisfied customer. She's been using Joan's service for two months.

'She's ruthless – twice she's found chocolate biscuits and thrown them out,' says Betty.

For further information please call:
Joan Smith (01492) 123456.

Business cards

Business cards help promote your enterprise, give the recipients confidence in you and give you credibility. If you are going to set up a money-making scheme, whether big or small, you should have business cards.

You can get simple designs, with black printing on white cards, made up by a local stationer or a print shop. If you are going to try this option, shop around and get quotations. There is a vast price differential among printers. What might cost you £25 at one shop will set you back £80 at another. Get three to five different quotations. Expect to pay £20–45 for 50–250 black-and-white cards with basic information.

Your cards should include:

- the name of your business
- your name
- your address
- business and after-hours phone numbers.

You might also consider listing on the card the services you provide, as well. However, try not to make the card look too full of information: take guidance from the printers as to what looks best.

Home-made alternative

Another alternative is to make your own business cards. Home-made cards can become conversation pieces and will probably get noticed more than traditional ones. Cards made from recycled paper will also get noticed. I know, because someone once gave me a business card made in this way, and I kept it longer than any other cards because it was unusual. A popular and easy way to make cards is to have a rubber stamp made up with your name and number.

Fliers

Fliers serve as a multi-purpose promotional device. They can be handed out at special events, used for letter-box drops, put under car windscreen wipers, handed out at markets, included with an item when sold, or sent to prospective clients – and, you'll need lots of them. Here are some tips for making fliers.

Information

Make sure you include your business name, phone numbers, a contact name and a description of the type of service you offer. List starting prices and emphasise that you take orders. Make sure you use bold print on your flier to highlight key points. Fliers should be uncluttered, to the point and easy to understand. They can also include specials and introductory offers.

Size

Fliers should be A5, half the size of an A4 page, so they are easy to handle and to read.

Printing

Fliers that are half the size of an A4 sheet can be printed two to a page. Consider photocopying your fliers onto coloured paper to attract attention. You will find prices can vary greatly. Ring around to check for quantity discounts: try to maximise quantity and value for money.

Delivering the fliers

If your fliers are being used for letter-box drops, you'll need to enlist the help of friends or family. The more people available, the more fliers will be delivered. You might also want to consider paying local school students to deliver fliers. If your fliers are set out on your market stall, make sure they are readily accessible, and secure them so they don't blow away.

5

BUSINESS GIMMICKS

The business world is very competitive, so it helps in the age of computers, the Internet and changing work patterns to use some bang up-to-date business gimmicks to attract customers.

I don't mean wearing a funny hat or a costume to attract attention. Rather, think how you can make your business stand out and think how you can ensure the service or product you offer is just that little bit better than the next person's.

What can you do to attract attention to your business? The ideas in this chapter include:

- magnetic signs
- mobile phones, pagers and faxes
- mobile and dial-it services
- the Internet
- insurance.

Magnetic signs

An effective way of advertising your business is to put a magnetic sign on the side of your car. Everywhere you drive, people will see the sign. Those interested in your service are likely to give you a call. The signs are easily removed and leave no marks on the car. And the best thing is, once you purchase the sign the advertising is free because it's on *your* vehicle.

Your sign should be clear and easy to read. Make sure that the colours stand out and are complementary, and that the text is easy to read. It should include your business name and phone number.

A local sign-maker probably provides this service or, if not, can tell you who does. Ask your sign-maker about fridge magnets, too. They are a good way to advertise your business, and are ideal for encouraging repeat business. With one of your magnets on their fridge, clients will always have your number on hand.

— Mobile phones, pagers and faxes —

Modern businesses, small or large, are all about immediacy. You have to be contactable and available, especially if you are providing a service. If you can be contacted immediately, you are in a better position to provide a same-day service.

Being available when clients want you can often make or break the sale. I once interviewed a young man who had set up a window-cleaning business. He had put an advertisement in the paper giving his home phone number to contact. When he wasn't at home he hope-fully left his answering machine on, promising to ring clients back if they left a message. But instead of leaving messages, people were hanging up – they wanted immediate service. Once this man got a mobile phone, his business boomed – he was always contactable and clients loved that fact.

That's why it is important to invest in a mobile phone or a pager, especially if your business is one where people need immediate answers. Both devices give you and the customer easy access to each other. The mobile phone industry itself is very competitive, and there are good deals to be found. However, read the small print carefully and check on the conditions for disconnection if you find it doesn't suit you. Shop around. The point to remember is that the phone or pager is not an indulgence, it is a requirement for success.

You should also consider renting or buying a phone/fax machine. These two-in-one machines are excellent if your business requires you to fax clients information, or you need to receive information.

—— Mobile and 'dial-a- ... ' services ——

Many of the money-making ideas in this book address the needs of extremely busy people. People have less and less spare time, so services that offer to come to them at home or at the office are growing in popularity.

It's not just people working outside the home who find it difficult to get out to pay bills, have their hair cut, have the car cleaned or have a facial. House husbands and wives are also busy. Many find it hard to get baby-sitters while they go shopping and, hence, are using mobile services more often.

The key to a successful mobile service is to make it affordable: emphasise in advertising that just because you're a mobile service does not mean you're more expensive. Set your rates at a level that is competitive with the non-mobile services. And watch your own costs – be sure to group appointments in the same geographic area to save time and to reduce travelling expenses.

—————————— The Internet ——————————

The Internet is fast becoming a valuable reserach tool for small and big businesses. You can use it to search for information relating to your business and to access news and the websites of government departments and small-business agencies. You can also establish your own small business website promoting your product. In fact, some small business operators sell their products via the Internet only.

For example, one lady offers advice about planning a wedding via the web; another man sells hot pasta sauces via the web – people e-mail their orders and he posts them out.

You can also find out valuable information by doing 'searches' on the Internet. What might take hours of trudging to libraries and bookstores and other advisory groups can be done in a few strokes of the computer keys. But be warned, you do need to be computer literate.

If you want to use the Internet for your business, you need to ensure your home computer is powerful enough to allow you to access the Internet. You will need to purchase Internet software and a modem.

Once you have done this, you will need to find a service provider to sign up with and buy access Internet time.

The best advice is to talk to the experts. Enrol in an Internet users' course at your local college or night school. You can also contact computer users' groups via the phone book or ask at your local computer store. Get as much information as possible and educate yourself so you can ensure using the Internet gives you the best returns.

Insurance

Society is becoming more litigious, so it is vital that you find out what your insurance cover should be, no matter what small business you set up. Remember, the onus will be on you to get and have the right cover.

If you are providing a product or a service for which you, your clients or any property are at risk of harm, you should consider taking out insurance. For example, if you are cleaning roof gutters, running aerobics classes, using your garage for storage or working as a tour operator, the chances are you will need insurance. Contact local insurance agencies or small-business associations for advice on whether you need insurance and, if so, what type. Remember, not having cover could put you in financial and legal jeopardy.

6

THE PERSONAL TOUCH

If you really want to make a business of baby-sitting, approach it from a professional point of view: set up a baby-sitting service that can offer your clients more than just one person as a baby-sitter. You will find the convenience of an agency more attractive than just working on your own.

What to offer

You will be offering a baby-sitting service, run by you and a few friends, preferably people experienced with children. The service allows clients to ring a central number and request a baby-sitter for a certain date. They can request a regular sitter or, if that one is unavailable, one of the other people on the list. Through the service, your clients will always have access to a reliable sitter.

What you need

- experience in taking care of children
- a group of friends, all experienced in child-care
- a way to contact all sitters – pagers are probably the cheapest way
- references from satisfied customers for all baby-sitters
- a phone, and a mobile phone or pager for the main coordinator
- fliers, business cards and leaflets detailing your rates and services

- a diary
- a receipt book
- T-shirts advertising your business

Getting started

Get a group of motivated, committed friends together. Decide who will be the main contact and equip this person with a mobile phone.

Potential clients will want to see references and – more frequently these days – a police check. Contact your local police station and ask how you can get a police check done voluntarily on yourself and your colleagues. This is a vital safety element to ensure the client is happy and that you do not hire someone with a criminal record, especially one relating to children. You need to set this in motion fairly early on, as police checks can take some time.

Advertise your service in local papers and perhaps send out press releases to the media. Posters and fliers at toddler groups, nursery schools, playgroups and day-care centres will also enable you to reach prospective customers. Addressing parents' clubs and other similar organisations is a good way of spreading the word. Notices in school newsletters will also help get the message across. You could also contact single-parents groups and tell them about your service.

Open a bank account for the baby-sitting service and put 50p–£1 (or some other mutually agreed amount) from every baby-sitting job into the account. This money can be used to pay for overheads such as for phones, pagers and advertising.

When you advertise be sure to promote the members of the service. Tell clients if the staff member is an experienced mother, is studying for a teaching degree, or has special first-aid or medical training. Do not undersell the talent within your service.

What to charge

This will depend on what the going rate for baby-sitting is where you live. But don't charge less than £5 an hour, especially if the sitter is mature or has special experience.

Remember, your client is buying security and peace of mind. You are promising that you will care for their child properly – don't let them down.

———— 2 Caring for the elderly ————

Society is ageing, and the need for people to care for the elderly is also growing. The British Government and many European countries identify this as one of the current growth areas for jobs.

If you have cared for a relative or someone who is disabled, then this is a service that could suit your skills. Consider this as one way of making money – start a 'Dial-a-carer' service.

What to offer

You'll care for elderly or infirm people when their main carer needs the afternoon off, has to go out or needs a break. You will go to the person's home and stay with him/her. If you have few responsibilities yourself, you can also offer an overnight or complete weekend care service.

What you need

- experience in caring for the elderly
- a first-aid certificate
- a résumé or CV (and later, letters of appreciation from satisfied customers)
- a phone and a mobile phone or pager
- business cards, fliers and leaflets detailing your rates and services
- a diary
- a receipt book

Getting started

It is important to have some experience caring for the elderly or the infirm. If you have been a nurse or nurse's aide, you may find this a good way of earning money. Anyone starting up this sort of business should do a reputable first-aid and/or carer's course. Keep your skills up to date.

To let people know about your service, place an advertisement in the local paper. Contact local age-care organisations and let them know about your service. Provide them with a list of your rates and some fliers they can hand out. In your advertising and fliers, emphasise your first-aid training and highlight any experience you have in caring for the elderly. Also mention on your fliers that references are available. People should have confidence in your ability to look after your charge properly.

Contact any senior citizens' groups in your area and let them know you are available. You should also contact sports and social clubs in your area: club members may be caring for elderly relatives and may appreciate hearing from you.

Contact church groups and women's groups. Members of these groups may be caring for elderly relatives themselves or may know of people who could use your services. If you are a member of such a group, why not hand out leaflets at meetings or put up posters on the notice board? See if you can leave some fliers in doctors' waiting rooms.

What to charge

If you are looking after someone for a few hours you should charge by the hour. Consider asking £10 an hour.

If you have to care for someone overnight or for a full weekend you should quote a day or a weekend rate. Consider asking £40 for a day and £100 for a weekend.

Important fact

This is not a job to be taken lightly and if you have no experience caring for the elderly then do not attempt it. The elderly and infirm have special needs and the carers who work with them must be trustworthy and knowledgeable.

—— 3 Mobile nail care and facials ——

Modern women are returning to the work-force and have very little time to indulge themselves with a visit to the manicurist. At the same time, people who work at home are busy, and making the time for a trip to the beauty parlour can be difficult. So in both cases, a beauty parlour that comes to you is a great idea.

What to offer

You will be offering a mobile nail care and facial service. This means you'll go to people's homes or offices to do their nails or give them a facial. If you have the skills or experience, you should also offer a make-up service. This is a particularly good service for wedding parties, twenty-first birthdays and hen nights.

What you need

- experience as a manicurist or beautician – there are many short courses available but make sure they are reputable
- your own beauty kit – including equipment and products for nail sets, nail fills, facials and make-up
- a display book showing your course certificates and/or examples of your work, including photos of nails and make-up you have done
- your own car
- a magnetic sign for your car door
- insurance – check with your insurer whether you need cover
- a phone and a mobile phone or pager
- business cards, fliers and leaflets detailing your rates and services
- a diary
- a receipt book
- a T-shirt advertising your business

Getting started

You'll need to have completed a beauty course. Talk to beauticians and manicurists to find out which courses they rate highly. Make sure the course covers nail and hand care, make-up and face care. There are numerous beauty schools and adult education centres you can contact. Ring around and tell the schools exactly what you want. Compare prices for courses and find out what you will be taught. Make sure you come away from the course with a worthwhile qualification.

Once you have completed the course, start advertising in the paper in both the beauty and wedding sections. Put signs up at the local shopping centre and leave leaflets at nursery schools, schools, sporting clubs, church halls and social groups. In your leaflets, emphasise that you can come to the home or the office, and that people using your service need not have a special occasion to attend.

You might want to consider offering start-up specials like a half-price beauty 'pick-me-up'.

Let bridal boutiques know about your service and offer a discount for client referrals. Contact wedding organisers and leave leaflets and business cards with them.

What to charge

Aim at making your fees match those of local beauty shops. Take into account your travel and beauty supply costs. However, remember that you don't have the overheads of shop rental, power and other costs. This can give you a competitive edge on price. You also offer the advantage of a 'home service', which many women will welcome. Suggested start rates for your fees are listed below.

- manicure – £15–20
- nail set – £40–50
- mini-facial – £15–20
- deluxe facial – £25–35
- formal make-up session – £40–50

4 Dial an office massage and aerobics class

Office workers and computer users know what it's like to develop neck and back pain. I, for one, would love to receive a deep tissue massage once a week at the office. Others may want to relieve their stress at a lunch-time aerobics work-out. If you are a qualified massage therapist or an aerobics instructor, consider setting up a mobile service for offices and large companies in your town or city.

What to offer

You will go to offices to give clients neck and shoulder massages. Alternatively, you will hold lunch-time or early-morning work-out classes or perhaps organise power walking or running.

What you need

- massage or aerobics qualifications
- transport
- insurance
- a portfolio containing references
- fridge magnets
- a massage table or a chair (for massage service)
- a ghetto blaster and music tapes (for aerobics service)
- a phone and a mobile phone or pager
- business cards, fliers and leaflets detailing your rates and services
- a diary
- a receipt book
- a T-shirt advertising your business

Getting started

First, you'll need to have done a reputable course in massage or aerobics instruction. Then you can advertise your service in the paper. Contact social organisers and occupational health and safety officers at all the big offices in your area. Offer to visit the offices and demonstrate aerobics classes or massage. Ask if you may put up posters and leave business cards in communal areas. A leaflet drop in the car parks of major office blocks is a good idea. Leaflets may be slipped under the car windscreen wipers.

Put posters up at colleges, universities and adult education centres. Staff and researchers may be interested in using the massage service as well. Also consider contacting senior citizens' groups, schools, hospitals and other organisations that may be interested in your service.

Once your clients' colleagues see the massages you are giving, they'll probably want one as well – an easy way to pick up new business.

For aerobics classes, tell the main organisers the minimum class size and the charge per person. They can then organise the location and numbers – all you have to do is show up with some music and instruct.

You should also talk to your insurance agent about suitable insurance cover for your business. Take out a public liability policy which will cover you if you go into someone's office and break something or cause some form of damage. For cover for an injury in your class, each insurer has different criteria you must meet. Discuss this policy with your insurance agent.

What to charge

For massages, start your fees at around £12–15 per half-hour. For the aerobics class, set your fee at around £25 per half-hour session, so the more people who attend the cheaper the cost for each person.

As much as possible, try to block together appointments at the same company, so you can spend just a few hours at any one location. By doing so, you'll save time and energy, and avoid travelling all over town for a few hours' work.

5 House-sitting

An excellent way to earn extra cash during the holiday season is to house-sit. With burglaries on the increase, house security is high on any home-owner's agenda. When you house-sit, you are essentially providing the owner with peace of mind. These days, many people are willing to pay for the knowledge that their home is safe.

What to offer

You will be offering to stay in your clients' homes while they are on holiday. You will care for their plants, pets and house. You will be responsible for bringing in the mail and papers, and making sure the house is secure. This is a job which requires your clients to place a great deal of trust in you – you must act responsibly at all times.

What you need

- integrity, reliability and trustworthiness
- phone, mobile phone or pager
- spare time, especially over holiday periods
- experience in the security field would be an added bonus
- fridge magnets
- recommendations and references that can be easily checked
- a phone and a mobile phone or pager
- business cards, fliers and leaflets detailing your rates and experience
- a diary
- a receipt book

Getting started

Start by advertising in the local paper. Contact local travel agents and tell them about your service. If you can provide them with references and letters of appreciation from happy clients they may be willing to put your name on file and hand out fliers or tell clients about your service.

You could contact the local neighbourhood watch committee and tell them about your service. They may have members who would feel happier if someone were staying at their houses while they were on holiday.

Try animal boarding kennels – many people leave pets there when they go away. The kennels may consider letting you put up a poster, or accept some fliers for their clients. Tell community groups and local organisations about your service. Fliers and letter-box drops will also help spread the word.

Consider getting a police check done on yourself to prove to clients you have no criminal convictions. People are always very concerned about leaving someone they do not know well in charge of their home and in the past, rip-off merchants have set up these types of businesses as a front for organised house break-ins.

In all your advertising, emphasise that you have experience and references – people must have confidence in your service. You must also convince them of your absolute integrity. Leaving one's house in another's care is something most people do not take lightly.

What to charge

When setting a fee, remember you will be living in the person's house – your client will be paying for your rent, power and local phone calls. Charge either a weekend, a weekly or a monthly rate depending on how long your client will be away. Consider charging:

- weekend house-sit – £50–60
- week-long house-sit – £60–120
- month-long house-sit – £200–350

— 6 Bill-paying and errand service —

I am the sort of person who hates standing in line for anything, and if I am paying a bill, I will avoid a queue like the plague. It seems the person immediately in front of me is always the one who takes the longest to have his/her bill processed. Consequently, I started using a bill-paying and errand-running service. These courteous and kind people pay my bills, pick up my dry-cleaning and even post my mail. They are a godsend – I just don't know how I got by without them.

What to offer

You will be paying people's bills, picking up dry-cleaning, posting letters and even waiting in line for concert tickets.

What you need

- patience
- character references to demonstrate to new clients your credibility and trustworthiness
- transport
- a phone or pager
- business cards, fliers and leaflets detailing your rates and services
- a diary
- a receipt book
- a T-shirt advertising your business

Getting started

Put an advertisement in the paper and write a press release for the local media about your unique service. They may be interested in running a short 'human interest' piece. In the press release make sure you point out this is a service that is a modern-day must. Why should people wait in queues when you'll do it for them?

Posters at local shopping centres will help promote your business. Contact professional organisations and tell the members about your service: these people normally don't have the time to pay their bills in person.

Make sure you get personal references from satisfied customers. You can build up a portfolio to show to prospective clients.

Don't forget, letter-box drops are a good idea. Make contact with local businesses, especially those that employ large numbers of people. They all have internal newsletters and notice boards where you can place advertisements.

What to charge

You should charge by the hour but at a declining rate – £10 for the first hour, £8 for the next and £5 for the next. Also set a minimum time fee, so no matter how small the job you are guaranteed a certain fee.

———— 7 Grocery shopping ————

You would be surprised how many people – even in the area close around you – are too busy to shop. They may find it hard to find the time, or they may be housebound. Either way, they miss out on the bargains in the big supermarkets. So, why not set up a grocery-shopping service for this niche market?

What to offer

You will offer to shop for the items on the client's grocery list and deliver them. If the client goes out to work, you can offer to let yourself in and put the food away. You will also offer to watch for bargains to ensure your client gets best value for money. Emphasise that your service will save the client money. Instead of buying groceries each night at the corner shop, you'll shop for them at large supermarkets where prices are generally lower.

What you need

- your own transport
- character references
- knowledge of supermarkets and current prices
- an eye for bargains

- a phone and a mobile phone or pager, and an answering machine
- business cards, fliers and leaflets detailing your rates and services
- a diary
- a receipt book

Getting started

Advertise in the paper and send press releases to the local media. Tell them about your 'unusual' service. Posters at the supermarket and corner stores will also help spread the word. Put advertisements in internal staff newsletters of businesses and council offices in your area.

Consider leaving leaflets for working parents at nursery schools, day nurseries and childminding centres. Contact professional organisations in your area and tell them about your service. Senior citizens' groups may be interested in hearing from you. Letter-box drops will also attract attention. If you're really serious, get a magnetic sign made up for your car door – any publicity is good publicity.

What to charge

Charge around £10 for the first hour, then slightly less for each hour after that. Don't forget, senior citizen discounts will help drum up business.

———— 8 Birthday-gift shopping ————

I must confess I have a tendency to forget birthdays. The number of friends I have sent belated gifts and cards to grows daily. My intentions may be good, but my memory lets me down. Now I am sure there are thousands of people out there like me, people who would benefit from a gift-buying or card-sending service.

What to offer

You will be ringing your clients to remind them of their spouses', friends' and relatives' birthdays or anniversaries. You may also send out cards for them, buy gifts and ensure the right person gets the right gift, on the right day.

What you need

- a good knowledge of gift stores, sports stores and other places to buy presents
- a selection of greeting cards
- a résumé of your service and letters from satisfied customers
- transport
- a phone and a mobile phone or pager
- business cards, fliers and leaflets detailing your rates and services
- a diary
- a receipt book
- a T-shirt advertising your business

Getting started

Advertisements in local papers, notices in local authority newsletters and company newsletters will help generate business. Posters at shopping centres will also attract attention.

Contact professional organisations in your area. Ask them if you can advertise in their newsletter or if you can come to a meeting and hand out fliers. Clubs and organisations where people gather regularly are a great place to hand out fliers about your service. This is the type of service busy executives will like, so tap into as many papers and newsletters they are likely to read as possible.

Meet your clients face to face and get all their particulars – names, addresses, occasions, relationship to the person and so on.

Ask whether recipients get only a card or if they get flowers or presents as well. Find out what kinds of presents and flowers the client wishes to send. With a card-only service, get the client to write cards out at your first meeting, then you'll have a stock to send out in time, to arrive on the due dates. Payment for cards and flowers should be up-front. Protect yourself: you should spend other people's money, not your own.

What to charge

These are suggested charges only:

- card-sending, including local posting (card provided by client) – £2
- flower-sending (flowers paid for by client) – £5
- phone call reminders should be set at a flat fee to be paid at the first meeting, charge £1.50 per reminder call, including the cost of the phone call

9 Family modelling

We have all seen pictures of Elle, Linda Evangelista and Claudia Schiffer strutting along the catwalk – the very beautiful, modelling very beautiful clothes. But it may surprise you that not all models are drop-dead gorgeous.

Modelling agencies are always on the look-out for real people: babies, toddlers, mums, dads, aunts, uncles, grandmas and grandpas to do catalogue work and catwalk modelling.

What to offer

If your family or members of your family have that 'real look' you should send in photos and personal details to modelling agencies and ask them to represent you.

What you need

- photos of your family: head and shoulder shots and full-length shots
- CVs for each person, especially if they have had acting experience or have an unusual accent or talent
- a phone

Getting started

First send your photos and CVs to reputable agencies. You should then follow up your letter with a call and perhaps visit the agency. If they put you on their books they will send you to castings, which are actually auditions for jobs. Remember to take along a portfolio of photos and to ask the agency what they want you to wear for the call or casting.

Competition for all forms of modelling is tough but if you have that certain look the agencies want, you will probably enjoy some success. Always be pleasant and be on time for castings and jobs.

Remember that not all model agencies operating are reputable companies so be careful not to get ripped off. Ask if the agency is a member of your country's Association of Model Agencies and check their credentials.

In London the Elisabeth Smith Agency offers a hot-line people can ring for information about modelling. It tells them what will be required of them and the costs involved. You can call them on 0891 715 393, but note that this is a premium line number and the call may be expensive.

The Agency also can send out a special booklet on child and family modelling. It costs around £6 and you will have to provide a stamped self-addressed envelope. You can write to the agency at 81 Headstone Road, Harrow, HA1 1PQ. Remember, most agencies are very busy and get calls every day from people wanting to get into modelling, so write in first for information

When you meet an agency representative don't be pressurised into spending large amounts of money for photographs or inclusion in agency books. A reputable agent will give you a fair assessment of your chances in the modelling world and give you time to make your decision. Ensure that you find out about the agency's terms and conditions and the agent's fee. The point is to enjoy family modelling and not be pressured or ripped off.

What to charge

The agency will take a percentage of any fees you are paid, normally between ten and twenty per cent. You usually get paid four to eight weeks after the job.

Family rates are normally negotiated depending on the number of people and the type of job. For photographic work children aged between five and twelve get £45–60 per hour. Teenagers and adults can expect £65–90 an hour.

For fittings you will be paid about half the hourly rate and audition fees are around £15 an hour.

10 Restaurant deliveries

How many times have you wanted to order from a favourite restaurant, but discovered it doesn't make home deliveries? It can be a real let-down. So, if the situation is similar in your area, consider setting up a home-delivery service.

What to offer

You will be providing local restaurants with a home-delivery service.

What you need

- a car and suitable insurance
- magnetic signs for the side of your car
- five to seven restaurants willing to participate in your delivery service
- a float of about £40 in change
- a phone and a mobile phone or pager
- business cards, fliers and leaflets detailing your rates and services
- a diary
- a receipt book
- T-shirts or baseball caps advertising your business

Getting started

Make a list of five to seven restaurants in your area that serve a selection of cuisines, such as Thai, Chinese, Indian, French, Italian (and pizza), seafood, vegetarian and perhaps chicken. Then contact each of the restaurants individually. Find out if they have a delivery service and, if they don't, offer to be one.

Once you have a group of participating restaurants, have their menus printed on a fold-out leaflet. If you can't fit all their menus on the leaflet, have the restaurants pick out their most popular dishes. Then, start letter-box dropping around your area. Leave some of the leaflets at each restaurant to be handed out to customers or put in takeaway bags.

You should also advertise in the local paper, and perhaps send out press releases to the local media telling them about the service you are offering.

What to charge

Work out your fuel expenses and other car costs per delivery. Stick to a five-mile (ten-kilometre) radius so you can keep your costs down. Decide whether to charge the restaurants or their home-delivery clients – it may be easier to get the clients to pay the delivery cost. Charge a flat rate, whether it's around the corner or the other side of town. You can charge £3–6 per delivery. Take payment from the client for the food and delivery, and then pay the restaurant.

Important fact

When delivering at night be aware of your personal safety. If there are some areas in your delivery area you don't want to service because of recent violent attacks, tell the restaurants. Do not take any chances.

7

IF YOUR TALENT IS COOKING AND CATERING

First, a cautionary note

If you are intending to make a business cooking and selling your products for public consumption, you must check with your local authority or council's health department to see if their health regulations will affect where you make your products. You may need to have your kitchen checked and registered by health inspectors or you may be able to rent a restaurant kitchen after hours.

If you prepare food in your kitchen you need it to be inspected and approved. However, if you are using the client's kitchen then the law varies from country to country. The kitchen may not need local health inspector approval, but check to be sure.

Ring your authority for further information and remember the health inspector can arrive any time after the initial inspection to check health standards are being met.

1 Home-made cakes and pastries

Are you one of those people who cooks so well that friends and family are always suggesting you'd make a killing if you sold your products commercially? Well start listening and take their advice.

What to offer

You are offering to supply the local delicatessen with a regular weekly or twice-weekly batch of your favourite cakes and pastries. The food is home-cooked and must be made using fresh ingredients and a lot of love. One of your main selling points is that the products are home-made and unique. The food should taste 'just like mother made'.

What you need

- a good recipe with almost universal appeal
- a car, for making deliveries
- a phone and a mobile phone or pager, and an answering machine
- business cards, fliers and leaflets detailing your rates and services
- a diary
- an order book
- a receipt book

Getting started

Make a batch of your favourite food and take it to a delicatessen. Be sure to be generous with samples. Tell the owner you'd like to be a supplier and offer that batch free to sell as a test run. If the first batch sells well, then you may be asked to supply that delicatessen regularly.

What to charge

How much you get will depend largely on how much the ingredients cost you. Delicatessen owners will look at the goodies in terms of the number of separate pieces they can sell. Each piece will sell for 75p–£1.50 retail, depending on size and ingredients.

But be sure to confirm prices in your area by checking the prices of similar products sold in local delicatessens. Most gateaux, for example, will yield twelve or more pieces, so the minimum price you charge per item should be no less than £4–5.

Work out in advance how much your ingredients cost you and put a price on how long it takes you to make the product. Set a top price and an absolute bottom price you'll accept so you have some leeway for negotiation. You can also consider selling on consignment, in which case the retailer pays only for goods that are sold and returns any unsold goods.

--------- # 2 Home-cooked meals ---------

A common problem nowadays is having so little time to do so many things. By the end of the working day most people are tired out but they still have to summon the energy, enthusiasm and creativity to cook the evening meal. It can all be rather exhausting, but one solution is to have someone come in every night and prepare a meal. So, if you are good in the kitchen, consider offering a service like this.

What to offer

You will be letting yourself into the house at around 4.30–5.00 p.m. and preparing the family meal. Some families may want you to come only a few days a week, others may prefer you to come Monday to Friday. You'll prepare the meal and leave it ready on the stove, in the oven or microwave; or serve it to the family. You will also be responsible for helping plan the meals and will most likely do the shopping as well.

What you need

- excellent cooking ability
- transport
- a good recipe book
- expertise in family budget management
- patience
- character references
- a phone and a mobile phone or pager
- business cards, fliers and leaflets detailing your rates and services
- a diary
- a receipt book
- a T-shirt advertising your business

Getting started

The best way to get started is to put an advertisement in the paper. Contact professional groups in your area. Working mums would be particularly interested in hearing from you.

If possible, get together some personal references and some sample recipes. Then arrange to meet with prospective clients. Take a couple of sample dishes along – it breaks the ice, shows you are eager and gives the family a chance to sample your work. Find out the family's favourite dishes and whether any family members are on special diets.

What to charge

Work out a weekly fee based on the number of nights you prepare the meals. Make sure to include a charge for grocery shopping and any extra biscuit- or cake-baking you do.

Here is a list of suggested charges.

- meal-cooking Monday–Friday – £40–70, client supplies food
- meal-cooking (three nights) – £20–30 client supplies food
- meal-cooking and grocery-buying Monday–Friday – £50–80
- meal-cooking and grocery-buying (three nights) – £30–50

———— 3 Low-fat cooking ————

We all know watching your diet and losing weight can be tough – there is always the desire for a sweet treat that is not in the recommended food list. But if you do some research you will discover there are many low-fat cookbooks that offer great-tasting food without a high fat content.

What to offer

You will offer to supply local cafés and delicatessens with low-fat cakes, sweets and biscuits. This is a very up-to-the-minute service – delicious low-fat food that doesn't add the pounds. When promoting your product this is the pitch you need for success.

What you need

- cooking skills
- low-fat recipes
- a council-approved kitchen (or hire a restaurant's kitchen during their off-time)
- a phone and a mobile phone or pager
- business cards, fliers and leaflets detailing your rates and services
- a diary
- an order book
- a receipt book
- a T-shirt advertising your business

Getting started

Prepare a range of cakes and biscuits and take them to local delicatessen and café owners. Offer to give them a sample box including information about the fat content of all foods. This is your selling point – low-fat food that is fun to eat. You could also try setting up a stall at your local weekend market. Again, have business cards and fliers ready to hand out. You should also contact local diet groups and tell them of your service. Don't forget big companies and government departments. They may need trays of food supplied for special events and a low-fat tray may be something different to put on the menu.

What to charge

You must first determine how much your ingredients cost for each product. Work out how long the food preparation takes, and set a reasonable hourly rate, such as £10. Total it up, then add 50 per cent on top of that for your profit. Include in that calculation the cost of your time and delivery. Budgeting for a service like this is vital and you must always ensure you make a profit on every cake, biscuit or muffin you sell.

——— 4 Organic cakes and pies ———

People are becoming increasingly concerned about the effects of pesticides and other hazardous chemicals on fruit, vegetables and other foods. If you are a good cook, perhaps you should consider making cakes and pies using only organic products. You can sell these cakes and pies to cafés, restaurants and health-food stores.

What to offer

Offer to supply cafés, restaurants and health-food stores with cakes, pies and biscuits made exclusively from organic products. You can also sell these cakes and pies at weekend markets. When promoting your products, emphasise that they are gourmet organic cakes and pies, made using fresh, chemical-free ingredients.

What you need

- talent in the kitchen
- access to organic products including flours, sugars, fruits and vegetables
- a range of recipes for cakes, pies and biscuits
- transport, to deliver your baked goods
- a table, chair and umbrella for weekend market stalls
- a phone and a mobile phone or pager
- business cards, fliers and leaflets detailing your rates and services
- a diary
- a receipt book

Getting started

First decide on a small sample range of cakes, pies or biscuits. Then buy the organic products – make sure you get a letter from the seller to ensure that the products are organic. Show the letter to your clients. Make up a sample range and do the rounds of cafés, restaurants and health food stores. Leave them samples and offer to supply them on a regular basis.

You can try selling your goods at a weekend market. Remember, large posters and fliers will help you reach more customers.

Another option is to ask a local restaurant if you can hire their approved kitchen in their off-time to prepare your goodies. You should also consider offering an organic catering service for home and office parties. A service like this may appeal to the health-conscious.

What to charge

Keep a strict record of ingredient costs, phone calls and travel costs. Then add about 20–40 per cent profit for yourself on top of that. Remember, because your product is 'organic' you can charge a little more. A wholesale price of £5 for a basic cake for a café is a good starting point. Ensure you cover your costs and enjoy a reasonable profit.

5 Making party food

Successful parties often depend on good food and drinks but with people so busy these days, they do not have the time to prepare. If you are a good cook turn your talents to party food preparation.

What to offer

You will be going to people's homes one or two hours before the party and preparing the nibbles and food for the party. Then once the food is ready, you leave. The host comes home, relaxes and welcomes the guests!

What you need

- experience as a cook
- a good collection of party recipes
- an apron or a T-shirt with your business name on the front
- an emergency supply of party food (olives, crisps, nuts, pesto, capers, etc.)
- a mobile phone or a pager
- business cards, fliers and leaflets detailing your rates and services
- a diary
- a receipt book
- a T-shirt or apron advertising your business

Getting started

You need to spread the word about your talent with party food. Advertise in the local paper and put up posters at shopping centres. Visit local party-supply shops and tell them about your service – they may let you leave leaflets and put up a poster. Contact social clubs and community groups to tell them about your service. Posters and leaflets at toddler groups, nursery schools, playgroups and day-care centres are a must.

Large companies, such as law firms and accountancy groups, often hold parties; you should send them leaflets and price lists.

What to charge

Start at about £10–15 an hour, and more if you have to provide all the food or if you are required to do the shopping. If you prefer, charge a per party fee:

- small parties (up to 20 people) £30 excluding food
- medium parties (20–50 people) £50 excluding food.

6 Cake decorating

A beautifully decorated cake will often be the focal point of any celebration party. If you have a knack for cake decorating, by traditional methods or by using realistic images, you should think about setting up a small business making 'designer' cakes.

What to offer

You will be decorating cakes as one-offs. You will meet with the client to discuss their needs and ideas, and then decorate the cake they provide.

What you need

- experience as a cake decorator (if you feel this is the field for you but you need more experience, consider enrolling in an adult education course)

- decorating equipment
- a supply of top-quality icing sugar, creams, colourings, etc.
- plastic gloves
- a portfolio of photographs of cakes you have made, to show off your skills
- references from satisfied customers, once you have some clients
- a phone and a mobile phone or pager
- business cards, fliers and leaflets (artistic, to reflect your cake-decorating flair) detailing your rates and services
- a diary
- a receipt book
- a T-shirt advertising your business

Getting started

First consider your cake-decorating skills realistically. Take an adult education course to learn some new techniques and bring your old skills back up to speed, if you need to. Once you are ready to start your business, decorate some sample cakes and take photos for your portfolio. If you are very confident, consider approaching the local shopping centre or bridal store and ask if you can set up a display of completed cakes.

Advertise in local papers and contact bridal shops, wedding organisers, caterers and party-venue coordinators. Tell them all about your service and ask if you can leave fliers and business cards.

If you want to get media coverage, try sending a cake decorated like your local newspaper or shaped like a radio to the appropriate person. It just may get some attention and convince the media that your business is 'different' enough to warrant a story.

The aim is to get as many people as possible talking about your service. On your fliers make sure you emphasise that the service is personalised, and point out why your service is different.

Cakes that are becoming popular are those that are decorated with a painting of the person celebrating the birthday, or have an unusual shape. It helps if you consider the cake as your canvas.

You should also consider participation in craft and specialist fares to attract attention.

Offer clients a range of cake flavours – for example, try chocolate mud cake or carrot cake as well as traditional fruit cake.

What to charge

This depends on the size of the cake and the amount of work required. Charge for the cake base itself, i.e. the cake you decorate, then add on decoration costs. Wedding cakes should start at around £100 for a very basic model. Christening cakes and birthday cakes should start at around £50. Remember, do not underestimate your talent: charge accordingly.

— 7 Gourmet jams and chocolates —

Jams made from local produce or handmade chocolates in the shape of your region could be big winners with tourists and visitors. Locally made, locally produced and locally grown – these are all features which make people want to buy. Consider as well using only organic products as a further enticement to make people want to buy. If your talents lie in this area, it's time to cash in.

What to offer

You will be making jams from local fruit to sell at markets. You will also be offering jams to local restaurants and hotels for resale.

You will be making handmade chocolates to sell at markets and offering to make chocolates for large hotels and restaurants to have exclusively on their menus as local products.

What you need

- talent in the kitchen
- recipe books
- jam-making equipment and a good supply of local fruit
- a supply of chocolate
- chocolate moulds
- jam jars and fabric and ribbon for decoration
- cellophane bags and ribbon for the chocolates

- handmade labels for the jams and chocolates
- baskets for displaying your products to hotel managers and café operators
- table, chair and umbrella for markets
- a phone and a mobile phone or pager
- business cards, fliers and leaflets detailing your rates and services
- a diary
- an order book
- a receipt book
- a T-shirt or sweatshirt advertising your business

Getting started

First prepare a selection of jams and chocolates. Make sure they are well presented. Decorate the tops of jam jars with colourful fabric and ribbon. Put the chocolates in cellophane bags and tie with colourful ribbon. Hand-print labels and remember to include your phone number, the date the product was made and the use-by date.

Take your products around to local hotel operators, cafés and delicatessens and ask if they will serve them or stock them. You could offer to make chocolates, for example, in the shape of the hotel's logo, to be served with coffee after dinner.

A stall at the local weekend market is another ideal outlet for your products.

Consider making chocolates for weddings, birthdays and other special events. Show your chocolate range to wedding organisers, bridal boutiques and special-events caterers. Ask if they would recommend potential clients to you and be sure to offer a discount for referrals.

What to charge

Jams should sell for £3.50–8 depending on size and contents. The charge for the chocolates will depend on the quantity ordered and whether they are specially designed or made using your own moulds. Remember, because they are gourmet quality you can charge a little extra.

8 Making vinegars

With the demand for high-quality, home-made products, you can identify the possibility of a number of niche markets. One of the simplest products to make is herbal vinegar – it not only sells well but, if nicely presented, also makes a great kitchen decoration.

What to offer

You will be making herbal wine vinegars at home and selling them to delicatessens or at weekend markets. The product is home-made and uses only high-quality, fresh and – preferably – organic ingredients.

What you need

- a bulk supply of wine vinegar
- a supply of organically grown herbs
- a supply of chillies, garlic and small onions
- bottles (recycled, cleaned and sterilised)
- bottle caps or corks
- ribbon and fabric for the top
- stick-on labels
- recipes for different wine vinegars
- a phone and a mobile phone or pager
- business cards, fliers and leaflets detailing your rates and services
- a diary
- an order book
- a receipt book

Getting started

First gather together a collection of wine vinegar, herbs (basil, thyme and rosemary are the best), garlic, cloves and red chillies (whole). Get some old sauce bottles and thoroughly wash and sterilise them. You can also get bottles, caps, corks and heat or chemical sterilisation equipment from beer/wine-making shops.

Making the vinegars is easy. Mix and match the herbs, put them into the bottles, then cover them with wine vinegar. Cork or cap the bottles, cover the top of each bottle with fabric and tie it with a bow or ribbon. List all the ingredients on the label and add the bottling date. The vinegars taste better if they are left to stand for a month or so. Do a taste test on your products before marketing them.

Once you have a nice selection together, take them around to local delicatessens and see if any are interested in buying them. Also, book a stall at the weekend market and sell your vinegars there. Have a good supply of business cards and fliers to hand out to passers-by.

What to charge

Your price will depend largely on how much your ingredients cost. Make a list of all costs, including a cost for finding or buying bottles and caps, a cost for the time spent making the vinegars and the cost of your stall. Then add on another 30–50 per cent as your profit. At some local markets I've been to, vinegars have sold for up to £5 a bottle, but price yourself within the market. Remember you are offering gourmet, organic wine vinegars so push that fact as a marketing tool.

9 Making pesto, mustard or pasta sauce

People have limited time when it comes to housework, cooking and cleaning. At the same time, they do want good quality when they sit down to a meal, although it must be quick to prepare. People are willing to pay that little bit extra if the product meets their quality and convenience criteria, and home-made pasta and pesto sauces can almost certainly meet those criteria. If you have an extra special pasta sauce recipe, why not try turning it into cash?

What to offer

Using your special recipe, you will be making pesto, mustards or home-made pasta sauces, packed in plastic tubs for takeaway convenience. You will be selling the pesto and sauces to local delicatessens.

What you need

- a good pesto, pasta sauce or mustard recipe
- a supply of basil, herbs, mushrooms, mustard seeds, tomatoes, olive oil, parmesan cheese, garlic and other fresh ingredients
- mixing bowls and kitchen equipment
- plastic takeaway containers
- labels
- a date stamp (to mark the use-by date)
- aprons
- transport
- a phone and a mobile phone or pager
- business cards, fliers and leaflets detailing your rates and services
- a diary
- a receipt book

Getting started

First make a batch of pesto, mustard or pasta sauce and take it to local delicatessens. Leave some samples and tell them you are interested in supplying them regularly. Emphasise the fact that the product is home-made, from fresh ingredients. Also emphasise that your products make meal preparation quick and easy for busy people. Alternatively, set up a stall at your local market and attract customers this way.

What to charge

Your price will depend largely on your costs. Add the costs of all your ingredients, your time, the labels and plastic tubs. Add on about 50 per cent as your profit margin.

Success story

Tanya made great pesto and her friends encouraged her to take samples to the local delicatessen. She did and it sold like hot cakes. She ended up supplying 2000 delicatessens and spending £5000 on her own rented kitchen. Her business was an overnight success because she offered a high-quality home-made product with a catchy name – Tanya's Perfect Pesto. Although she knew there were other pesto-makers in the market, her personalised service made people want to buy from her.

—— 10 Diet checker and diet cook ——

For many people losing weight is a tough battle. But if they could hire someone to do spot-checks to make sure they are sticking to their diet, losing weight might be easier.

What to offer

You will be offering two types of service. The first entails dropping in on clients to see how their diets are going and to offer moral support. These visits will be unannounced, to make sure the person isn't hiding chocolate in the fridge.

Alternatively, you could spend a day or a half-day preparing a week's meals to be placed in the fridge or freezer. The dieter just has to microwave them or pop them in the oven.

What you need

- empathy with dieters and ability to communicate well
- transport
- experience in the kitchen
- a selection of low-fat, nutritious diet recipes
- transport
- a phone and a mobile phone or pager
- business cards, fliers and leaflets detailing your rates and services
- a filing system and a diary to keep track of clients and their various needs
- a receipt book
- a T-shirt advertising your business

Getting started

First advertise your services in the local paper – both as a diet cook/chef and as a diet checker. Then contact local weight-loss centres and, more importantly, local weight-loss support groups. Tell them all about your services, hand out fliers, advertise in their newsletters and offer start-up discounts. You should also contact local gyms and ask if you can put up posters and leave fliers and business cards.

They may have special weight-loss gym and aerobics classes where you can give a cooking demonstration or hand out fliers.

Posters and fliers at fruit and vegetable shops and health-food stores may also help to attract clients. Once you have a good base you can start collecting testimonials from various clients to put in your portfolio. You will also find the message spreading by word of mouth.

Give your clients your mobile number and tell them whenever they have a serious craving, to ring you rather than indulge. Then you can talk them out of the temptation to break the diet.

Don't forget to send out press releases to local media and weight-loss magazines. A story like this may catch the eye because it is such an unusual and personal service.

What to charge

Meal-cooking sample rates

- half-day – £60
- full day – £100
- shopping for produce – £10 an hour

Diet-checking sample rates

- four visits per week for two weeks – £40
- four visits per week for four weeks – £75

8

USING ORGANISATION-AL, SECRETARIAL AND TEACHING SKILLS

1 Personal organiser

Have you noticed, some people are just untidy and disorganised? If you happen to be good at organising other people's lives, then these are the people who need your help. It's a messy job but someone has to do it.

What to offer

You will offer to come into people's homes to tidy and colour-code their wardrobe, sort out their kitchen cupboards, redo their address and contact books, fix up photo albums and organise a good bill-paying system.

What you need

- organisational skills
- transport
- a phone and a mobile phone or pager
- business cards, fliers and leaflets detailing your rates and services
- a diary
- a receipt book
- a T-shirt advertising your business

Getting started

Tell as many people about your service as possible. Put an advertisement in the paper and in as many newsletters as you can gain entry to. Put up posters at local shopping centres. Contact sporting groups, gyms, professional organisations, women's groups and social clubs. Tell them all about your service and distribute leaflets to them. Make sure you send out a press release to media organisations – this is one of those jobs which is just wacky enough to get attention.

Your clients will expect you to do a number of things. Starting with their wardrobes, you'll need to tidy them and work out a storage system that suits the clients and allows them easy and quick access to their clothes.

Tidy kitchen and bathroom cupboards in the same way. Offer to update clients' address books; this will mean buying new ones and neatly rewriting all the information. Also offer to tidy up their photo albums and fix loose photos.

If your client is forgetful about bill paying, try to work out a system – which might include a pinboard and regular reminders about bills.

Have a list of reliable house-cleaners, window-cleaners, ironers and repairers you can pass on to your clients. If they are busy people they may ask you to coordinate the services of these people. Make sure the people you refer are good at their jobs and can be trusted.

What to charge

You should charge by the hour: £10–20 is a good base rate. If the job is going to take more than an hour, consider settling on a daily rate: £80–100 for an eight-hour day is a good starting point.

2 Organising and decorating for kids' parties

Children's parties are making a comeback. They are a chance for the kids – and their mum, dad and their friends – to have a good time. But as with everything nowadays, organising parties takes time.

An untapped niche market is organising kids parties and decorating the house for them. This need not be an outrageously expensive party coordinator, but simply someone who can help organise the party, make decorations and ensure that everyone has a good time.

What to offer

You will offer to organise or help with children's parties. You can take charge of the party invitations, cake, decorations, party favours and entertainment – or may simply come in to decorate the hall for the birthday celebration. The aim is to provide this service at a price the parents can afford, to ensure the success of the party.

What you need

- ability to get along with children
- an eye for detail and an artistic flair
- organisational skills
- streamers, party hats, etc.
- a portfolio with photographs of parties you have organised
- an ability to get discounts on party supplies
- magnetic signs to stick on the side of the car door
- a phone and a mobile phone or pager
- business cards, fliers and leaflets detailing your rates and services
- a diary
- a receipt book
- a T-shirt to wear at the party advertising your business

Getting started

First, attend as many birthday parties for kids as possible and talk to your friends and family about what is fashionable for children's parties. Current trends include serving organic food, and hiring pinball machines and computer games to keep kids entertained. Other popular ideas include a birthday celebration at a local theme park, and theme birthday parties. One very popular theme is 'The 21st Century', inspired by computer games.

Look for party books at your local newsagent or book store. Select those describing cheap and easy ways to make decorations or suggesting unusual forms of entertainment that will help make the birthday parties special. Also get hold of price lists from local fancy-dress hire shops so that you can have them available when the parents decide they want a theme birthday party. See if the fancy-dress shop will offer you a discount as a regular customer. Do the same with bakeries specialising in birthday cakes.

Parents will feel they are getting a bargain, and you'll be minimising your own costs.

To attract customers, put up posters at local child-care centres, play groups, schools and nursery schools. Hand out fliers to parents and, perhaps, address a parents' club meeting. Posters at the shopping centre will also help develop a client base. Referral by word of mouth is important. You can also take the opportunity to hand out fliers to other mums and dads at the party.

An advertisement in the local paper will get the phones ringing. Send a press release about your service to the media. You never know, they may be interested in running an article, especially if they can get some cute party pictures.

What to charge

Talk with the parents and ask them how much they want to spend on the party in terms of decorations, cake etc. Then, quote your fee for organising the entire party. Most kids' parties will take about eight hours to organise so charge £30–50 for your time.

If you are hired to decorate the room then charge about £8 an hour plus decoration costs. Most rooms will take you a minimum of two hours to decorate. Don't forget to take photos for your portfolio.

3 Flatmate finder

Finding a suitable flatmate can be a nightmare, especially if you are busy or are new to an area. Setting up interview times, vetting applicants and making sure the person is right for you can be tough. A central agency that vets applicants and matches the right house or flat to the right person but doesn't aim to rip people off can be profitable.

What to offer

You will be offering to find a suitable flatmate for people who have a room to let or sublet. You will also be offering to find the ideal house-sharing partners for people who want to rent a room.

What you need

- a computer to set up your database
- a filing cabinet and files
- application forms for people who will use your service
- a map of the area you will cover
- a room at your house to serve as an office for interviews
- a portfolio of happy clients and references
- a disclaimer document, waiving your client's right to sue you for any problems occurring as a result of flatmates you have recommended through the service
- insurance – check with your insurance agent regarding any cover you may need, in addition to the disclaimer
- a phone and a mobile phone or pager
- business cards, fliers and leaflets detailing your rates and services
- a diary
- a receipt book

Getting started

First advertise for both 'landlords' and 'tenants'. You need a range of rooms available to match up your prospective tenants. Advertise regularly in the paper. It will take a few weeks to build up your lists, but after that it should become easier to find the right people.

You will need an extensive application form for both 'landlords' and 'tenants'. They should list likes and dislikes, the kind of flatmate they are looking for, their habits, what time they leave for work, what their social schedule is like, and so forth. You don't want to match a non-smoker with a smoker or a strict vegetarian with a meat-eater.

Those who have rooms to rent should bring in photos of the house or flat and the room, for you to show to people during the initial interview.

You can vet potential tenants and check their references, and then give a list of four or five to the client with the room to let. The client can ring the potential tenants and organise a time to meet. Once someone moves in, the client offering the room pays you a finder's fee.

What to charge

Payment systems can vary. People with rooms to let should pay you a flat fee of £50–100 for the service. Someone searching for a room should pay the equivalent of one week's rent once you find them accommodation.

4 Typing

For this money-making scheme, you need a talent for word-processing. Typing for university students and for businesses is a way of earning some extra cash and you can stay at home while you're doing it. The important point to remember is to target your niche market and develop a good reputation.

What to offer

You will be offering to type assignments and thesis papers for students and documents for lecturers. You will also be offering to type letters and documents for small businesses in your area.

What you need

- a word processor
- a laser printer
- a small tape recorder for dictation purposes
- note pads, pens, typing paper and liquid paper
- an answering machine
- a phone and a mobile phone or pager
- business cards, fliers and leaflets detailing your rates and services
- a diary
- a receipt book

Getting started

First choose your market, depending on your abilities. Typing for undergraduates and businesses is relatively straightforward. But for many graduate students and professors, you may need to format to very precise specifications or type scientific or mathematics notations, Greek symbols and tables. Note that some word-processors include special mathematical facilities, or may have add-on accessories.

Next concentrate on getting together a list of regular clients. Advertising in the local paper is a good start. If you live near a university or adult education centre, put an advertisement in the student paper, pin posters up around the campus and place an advertisement in the staff newsletter. Perhaps you could place fliers in the mail boxes of the university lecturers. Also contact the student unions and tell them about your service.

If you develop a good reputation among students and academics you will find work will increase through word of mouth. Leave your posters up and continue to advertise in the local paper past the end of term and over the holidays. Many students will still have essays to complete and work which has been granted an extension. If you're lucky, the work should continue over university breaks.

To let business people know about your service try letter-box drops in the local business area. Also try door-knocking at some of the businesses in your area. Putting a face to a name will help to bring in business. Continue to advertise in the local paper and contact local business associations to tell them about your service.

What to charge

Charge by the page for small jobs. I suggest charging £1–2 for a page of straight typing. Work out a flat rate for larger jobs. Offer your clients the files on disk so that if they have a compatible system, they can make last-minute changes. You will need to ensure that the hardware and software you use is compatible with what your client uses. If you need to buy new equipment, take advice from computer magazines and sales staff to see what is commonly popular.

5 Career résumés (CVs) with a difference

Getting noticed in the work-force is, indeed, a tough job, but it's even tougher for those seeking that first job or getting an initial interview. Most employers ask applicants to send in a career résumé, or CV (*curriculum vitae*), which is then added to the growing pile.

So how do job seekers make sure their CV is the one employers sit down and read? They use your 'Career résumé-with-a-difference' service.

What to offer

You will be offering to help people design CVs that stand out and get noticed. This business is all about creative flair – if you have it then this is the job for you.

What you need

- creative flair
- a good imagination
- a computer
- pens, paper and other art equipment
- a supply of wacky ideas
- an office or second bedroom you can use as work space
- a portfolio showing the career résumés you have done
- a phone and a mobile phone or pager
- business cards, fliers and leaflets detailing your rates and services
- a diary
- a receipt book

Getting started

Designing résumés with a difference is a bit like working in public relations, where you have to come up with the right campaign for the right product or event. Here you have to come up with the right résumé for the right job.

I recently met a man who had sent a shark hook in a box with his résumé to an advertising company he wanted to work for. His line: he wanted to hook some work. He followed it up with a fishing line and his résumé, saying he wasn't spinning the employer a line, and was ready to be reeled in. Clever and witty – and, yes, he got the job.

A friend of mine sent a toy arm with his résumé, saying he would give his left arm to work for the company. One woman sent her résumé in book form covered with beautiful hand-drawn insects and ants, saying she was 'bugging' the company for some work. Another person sent in a résumé in book form – the diagrams were beautiful and simply caught the right person's attention.

One man had his résumé and photo professionally printed on glossy card so it could be turned into a fold-out – very clever and very professional.

This is the sort of innovative approach that a résumé-with-a-difference service needs. You need to be able to come up with a list of ideas that suit your client's personality and the job for which he/she is applying.

To get experience, you must try out your ideas. Talk to friends and relatives and prepare unusual résumés for them. Perhaps you have some friends who are actually applying for jobs and will use your résumé. You can then get references from them. The main benefit is that you will get vital feedback on what does and doesn't work.

Remember, the ideas must suit the job, otherwise the scheme may backfire.

To tell people about your service, start by advertising. Also try the local Job Centre or job-finding agencies. Or, perhaps you could hand out leaflets to people as they leave the Job Centres.

Contact head-hunting organisations and see if they can use your services. Career reference centres, university and adult education job counsellors are also good contact points. They may allow you to put up posters or agree to give your business cards to clients.

A creative press release using one of your résumés-with-a-difference techniques may also help generate some publicity. With this sort of business, your imagination is the only limit.

What to charge

Charge a consultation fee and an additional fee for making-up the résumé package. Start your consultation fees around the £20–30 mark. Charge an hourly rate for making-up the résumé, with material being extra.

Important fact

One point to remember is that the résumé must be truthful. The CV should give accurate details of what the person has done, in the work field, so far. You can stretch the truth, or even embroider it, but never lie, even if your client asks you to. Eventually the truth will out, and it could reflect on you.

—— 6 Community newsletter ——

Most communities have a major newspaper but smaller areas within that community may also benefit from a regular newsletter. If you have writing ability this might be an option for you.

What to offer

You will write a weekly or monthly community newsletter for your neighbourhood. You will produce it on your home computer and sell advertising.

What you need

- journalistic ability
- a computer
- a photocopier
- the ability to sell advertising
- people to help with letter-box drops and stores that will distribute your newsletter
- a phone and a mobile phone or pager

Getting started

First of all this newsletter is very different from the local newspaper. It will target a certain area of the community, either in interests or location.

Start small – for example with a four-page newsletter. Find some local stories that you know will interest your market. Include a diary about forthcoming events, rubbish and recycled paper collection times, school holiday dates – basic household information that people find valuable.

Then contact local businesses and encourage them to advertise. Tell them clearly who the market is and why advertising with you will be a benefit. Show them a mock-up of the newsletter. If they advertise perhaps they would also agree to let you leave some of the newsletters on the counters of their shops as a means of distribution. As you won't charge people to buy the newsletter, you want to make your profit from advertising.

Once the newsletter starts you can also take advertising from people having garage sales, wanting to sell products etc.

Keep your first run small. It's best to print off a master copy and then photocopy it and distribute via letter-boxing and through the newsletter being available at local stores.

This small business requires stamina and perseverance. People love to know what is going on in their local area and if you provide that information in your newsletter you will find businesses will advertise.

In the area I live in, two mums got together and put together a newsletter like this. It started small – one A4 page folded in half – and is now a genuine growing concern. People say their publication is the most widely read in our area because it is so local in content. Its owners are making money through advertising and found classified advertising to be a big money spinner. Their suggestion is not to try to compete with newspapers, but to make your newsletter special so that people want to read it.

What to charge

Work out what your advertising rates will be. For example a boxed advertisement, one column wide and five centimetres deep, may cost

£20. Classified advertisements should be charged per word or per line; perhaps you could offer the first line free as an incentive to advertisers.

——— 7 Family tree history writer ———

If you are good at finding out information and then writing succinct and interesting accounts, then perhaps this is the money-making scheme for you. There is a growing interest in researching family trees; however, research can be tough and time-consuming, and then once the information is found there's no time to write it all down and put it into one cohesive 'historical' document. That's where you come in.

What to offer

You will be offering a family tree research service. This will involve researching people's family origins and then collecting all the information into a spiral-bound folder or book.

You can also offer an interview service involving talking to key family members about their lives and family origins. The interviews can be recorded on a cassette or on video tape for posterity. The thrust of this type of service is not letting family history die out.

What you need

- research skills
- an ability to talk easily with people
- notepad, pens, etc.
- a reliable tape recorder or video recorder, with a microphone for interviews
- access to a spiral-binder machine to turn your research into a family history book
- files for your various researches
- business cards and leaflets detailing your rates and services
- a diary
- a receipt book

Getting started

First, develop a list of organisations that can help you research family trees. Start with the local genealogical society in your town or city and contact the registrar of births, deaths and marriages and any history groups in your town that might keep records you can use.

Then start with an advertisement in the paper and posters at shopping centres. Contact women's groups, sporting organisations and senior citizens associations.

Try to get approval to put up posters at the registry of births, deaths and marriages. You should also put signs up at the local library and the local cemetery because these are both places where many people go to get information. If you are computer literate there are a number of family history programs you can buy which can help your research and also provide a layout for attractive pages. Don't forget that the Internet can yield valuable historical information.

England and Wales
The General Register Office
Postal Applications Section,
Room 09
Smedley Hydro
Trafalgar Road
Southport
Merseyside PR8 2HH

Scotland
Registrar-General
New Register House
Edinburgh EH1 3YT

Northern Ireland
Registrar-General
Oxford House
49–55 Chichester Street
Belfast BT1 4HI

Irish Republic
Registrar-General
Joyce House
8–11 Lombard Street East
Dublin 2

Genealogy societies
Society of Genealogists
14 Charterhouse Buildings
Goswell Road
London EC1M 7BA

**Federation of Family
 History Societies**
The Benson Room
Birmingham & Midland Institute
Margaret Street
Birmingham B3 3BS

Scottish Genealogy Society
15 Victoria Terrace
Edinburgh EH1 2JL

Irish Family History Society
PO Box 36
NAAS
Co. Kildare Eire

What to charge

Your rates will depend largely on what the family wants you to do and how long it takes. Here are some suggested fees.

- basic family tree research going back four generations: £50–70 (excluding phone costs, faxing etc.)
- written family history, including collection of photos, spiral-bound: £75–150 (for the first copy)
- recorded interview including cassette: £20 per interview (If you video the interview your fees should start at around £50 an hour.)

These fees are meant only as a guide and will depend largely on how long you spend on each assignment and how easy it is to find the information you require.

You should also take into account the fees charged by registries for copies of certificates.

———————— 8 Tutoring ————————

This is a job suited to those who have tertiary qualifications or expertise in a certain field. Tutoring is in demand by parents who want their children to be helped with school work, by senior students studying for final examinations, and by university students needing help with their coursework.

What to offer

You will offer tutoring in the home for students needing help with their studies.

What you need

- experience or tertiary qualifications in the subject you are offering to tutor
- up-to-date reference material and appropriate textbooks
- a phone, an answering machine or a mobile phone
- your résumé, references and copies of your degree
- business cards
- a diary
- a receipt book

Getting started

First decide who you will be tutoring. Pick your market: primary school students, junior high students, senior high students, adult education students or university students.

Next put an advertisement in the paper and in any local publications which service the market you're tutoring.

For example, if you are targeting university or adult education students, put an advertisement in the student paper. Put signs up around local colleges and campuses and contact their student union. It wouldn't hurt to contact lecturers and teachers and ask if you can be of any assistance.

If school students are your target market, contact the schools and send in a letter and CV to the principal. They may agree to let you advertise in the school newsletter. Parents' associations are also another way to spread the word. Contact local associations, tell them about your service and show them your CV and references.

Remember, tutoring is all about listening to the needs and problems of your client. It is important that they tell you what their major problems are and what they hope to achieve through tutoring. Don't forget to get references from satisfied clients.

What to charge

You should charge by the hour. Your rates should reflect your level of experience and expertise. It should also reflect who you are tutoring. Primary-school students should be charged less than university-level students because the degree of preparation required is slightly less. I suggest setting your hourly rate at £20–30.

—— 9 Microwave cooking lessons ——

Are you a whiz with the microwave oven? If so, you are probably in the minority. Most people only use their microwave oven to defrost food and warm coffee. For many people, proper use of a microwave oven rates up there with the mysteries of how to program their VCR.

Why not take advantage of this lack of knowledge and teach people how to make the most of their microwave ovens? It is a niche market that has been largely unnoticed.

What to offer

You will offer to come to people's homes and give them one-to-one microwave cooking lessons. You can also offer to teach three or four friends together. You can offer a casual party-type atmosphere, over morning or afternoon tea or at night. Because you offer the convenience of going to people's homes, they will be more likely to take you up on the offer.

What you need

- experience and expertise in using a microwave oven
- a lesson plan
- a microwave oven
- transport
- a microwave instruction booklet, self-written, including recipes
- a phone and a mobile phone or pager, and an answering machine
- business cards, fliers and leaflets detailing your rates and services
- a diary for keeping track of lesson times and visits
- a receipt book
- a T-shirt advertising your business

Getting started

First, make a rough lesson plan. Keep it simple, explaining how a microwave oven works and which foods microwave well and which don't. Set out a basic guide for cooking common dishes such as roast beef, roast chicken, casseroles, vegetables, cakes and desserts. Include some of your favourite recipes. This will take a little bit of work on your part, but will be worth it.

Four or five pages of notes is all you need. You can photocopy them for your clients. Remember, your copyright automatically applies to such work. Be sure to include time conversions for ovens of various wattages: lower wattages will require longer cooking times.

Be aware that the course notes are only a guide. The nature and development of your courses will be determined largely by feedback from clients.

Before going into business, you'll probably want to try out your course on a few friends or neighbours for experience. Then advertise in the paper and, perhaps, put some signs and posters up at the supermarket and other food stores. Contact community groups, women's organisations and sporting clubs. Most will have newsletters in which you can advertise. Better still, offer to give a short presentation at their next meeting and then pass around a clipboard so people can sign up. Perhaps you can give lessons at the meeting.

Consider getting a T-shirt or sweater printed with the name of your course on it and a picture of a microwave oven. Also, contact manufacturers of microwave ovens and tell them you teach microwave cooking lessons. They may have some helpful cooking tips or promotional recipe booklets you can hand out.

When you complete a course, ask the group or individuals to write a reference for you or have them fill out evaluation sheets. Use these sheets to find ways to improve your course. If they are favourable, you can also show them to prospective clients.

What to charge

You should charge by the hour and per client. To start off, set your prices at about £15 an hour. If you are teaching a group of three or more, charge each client £9–12 so they feel they are getting a discount. When you set your prices, remember to take your travel time into account. Teach in an area that is within a small radius of your home to keep travel costs down.

——— 10 Computer help-line ———

Many homes nowadays have a computer, and children are taught to use them in school from an early age. But what happens at 9 o'clock in the evening, when they have a problem with their computer program and they have to hand in the project the next morning – who are they going to call? And how about the person who buys a computer but can't work out how to get the best from it? Have you read the manuals they come with? You need a computer science qualification to read the first page!

So if you – or perhaps your son or daughter – are a computer whiz, why not set up a home computer help-line?

What to offer

You will be offering to visit clients' homes to help them with their computer problems.

What you need

- expertise in using a computer or a particular computer system (You may have taken computer courses, have a university degree in computer science or just have a natural ability when it comes to using computer systems.)
- a library of computer manuals
- transport for home visits
- a note-book to record mileage in your car unless you use public transport
- recommendations and references
- fridge magnets
- a phone and a mobile phone or pager
- business cards, fliers and leaflets detailing your rates and services
- a diary
- a receipt book

Getting started

To attract clients, put an advertisement in the paper telling people about your service. Put up posters around university and college campuses. Contact local computer software and hardware stores, and computer clubs in your town or city. Local schools may also be interested in hearing from you and may let you advertise in their student paper. Don't forget community poster boards or notice boards at major shopping areas.

What to charge

For home visits, charge around £20 an hour. This will cover your travel time, your car expenses and the fee for your expertise.

Important note

To make a success of this type of business, you do need to know about computers across the board, not just be fairly good with one application. It might be an idea to get together with several other computer buffs, and then offer a more comprehensive service.

9

SELLING AND RENTING

━━━━ 1 Selling essential oils ━━━━

The use of essential oils is becoming increasingly popular. Pop stars, actors, royalty and everyday people now use them to help relieve a range of ailments, to give them an energy boost or to help them relax. So why not turn essential oils into your own small business success story?

What to offer

You will be selling small bottles of essential oils, massage oils and essential oil packs at local markets.

What you need

- experience with aromatherapy
- bulk supply of essential oils
- a supply of small bottles with droppers
- labels
- essential oil and massage oil recipes
- market stand
- a float of about £50 in change for market day
- a phone and a mobile phone or pager
- business cards, fliers and leaflets detailing your rates and services

- a diary
- a receipt book
- a T-shirt or sweatshirt advertising your business

Getting started

First do a short course in aromatherapy and research the topic as fully as possible. Then find a bulk supplier of oils and buy what you think you need. Put the oils into small bottles with droppers and label them. Mix up some massage oils using different aromatherapy recipes. For example soya oil and macadamia oil essence makes a good massage oil.

Make up some small aromatherapy packs. For example a romance pack should include three small bottles containing lavender, cedarwood and orange. An energy pack contains grapefruit, rosemary and peppermint. A chill-out pack contains orange, rosewood and clary sage.

What to charge

This will depend on your costs. Keep meticulous records of how much your bulk oils cost, and the prices of the small bottles and your set-up costs. Small bottles of oils should sell for £2–5 each. Your packs should sell for £5–15 each, depending on your costs and the competition.

2 Hamper selling

Hampers are great gifts for all sorts of occasions, including Christmas and birthdays, a baby hamper when someone gives birth, a christening hamper or a wedding hamper. If you have an eye for detail and love shopping, hamper selling is for you.

What to offer

You will be offering to put together hampers for special occasion gifts. You will sell the hampers at local markets.

What you need

- a range of baskets from a wholesaler
- a range of hamper contents – Christmas, birthdays, baby births, christenings, office going away etc.
- decorations for the hamper
- stickers for hampers advertising who made them
- a market stall
- a float of £50 for a market stall
- a phone and a mobile phone or pager
- business cards, fliers and leaflets detailing your rates and services
- a diary
- a receipt book
- a T-shirt advertising your business

Getting started

The first thing to do is put together a sample range of perishable and non-perishable hampers. These should be suitable for a range of occasions and suit different price ranges. Contact wholesalers to try to get the best deal on products.

For example in your baby hamper you might include baby clothes, nappies, pins, baby powder and lotions, dummies etc. A 21st birthday hamper for a woman might include sweets, cakes, a scarf, a gift voucher at a popular music store, some earrings and perfume.

Once you have a selection together set up your market stall. Make sure people know you take orders.

What to charge

This will largely depend on the cost of putting together each hamper. Remember to add a profit margin of 20–50 per cent.

3 Selling clothes from the 60s (and 70s)

As fashion turns full circle, outfits from the 1960s and 1970s are making a comeback. So why not cash in by raiding your cupboards and friends' cupboards and selling the old gear?

What to offer

You will be selling clothes from the 1960–70s, at a stall at a local market.

What you need

- a supply of 60s and 70s outfits in good condition
- a washing machine and an iron
- wire hangers and a clothes rack for the market stall
- a phone and a mobile phone or pager
- business cards, fliers and leaflets detailing your rates and services
- a diary
- a receipt book
- a T-shirt advertising your business

Getting started

First get together a supply of old clothes from your relatives and friends. Try garage sales and charity shops, too, to see what you can pick up. They may be willing to sell you boxes of clothes for a lot less than the total price of the individual items. You may want to specialise in a particular style of clothing. If so, you must always be on the look-out for possible supplies.

Once you have got the clothes together, wash them and iron them. In the case of shoes, polish and clean them. Then take the gear to the market. Take along plenty of change, as well as bags for customer purchases. Don't forget to include a business card in the bag with each item you sell – the more advertising the better.

What to charge

Visit local markets to check current prices, and set yours accordingly.

---
4 Selling bric-a-brac

Have you ever been to a market and seen a bric-a-brac stall? Stall owners sell a range of items such as crockery, silverware and 1950–60s odds and ends. Market-goers are fascinated by such products and collecting 'kitsch' is certainly growing in popularity.

What to offer

You will be selling odds and ends at a market stall.

What you need

- a selection of odds and ends (hints on where to find them later)
- a table and a chair for your market stall
- a float of £50 in change
- transport
- a phone and a mobile phone or pager
- business cards, fliers and leaflets detailing your rates and services
- a diary
- a receipt book

Getting started

The best way to find out what is selling is to check out the markets and see what is available at odds-and-ends stalls. Talk to market organisers. They are usually full of useful information about what is hot and what is not.

Next go through your own cupboards and pull out everything that you don't need any more – trinkets, crockery, cutlery etc. Then ask your relatives to do the same. This collection will form the basis of your stall merchandise.

Make up a flier offering to buy people's odds and ends and do a letter-box drop in your neighbourhood. Neighbours will probably be interested in selling to you because it saves them the bother of holding a garage sale. Remember you have to sell the goods at a profit so do not offer too much!

You should also try clearance sales at farms. You can usually pick up boxes of crockery and trinkets very cheaply because you pay by the box, not by the individual item. You may also be able to pick up bigger goods such as chairs which you can resell successfully.

What to charge

The rule with selling at markets is always to make some degree of profit. Do not undersell. Check out other stall holders' prices and always be prepared to haggle. Make sure you tag all the goods with their prices, but also put up a poster saying 'Make me an offer'. This approach encourages people to haggle and tells them the price you are quoting may not be the price they will pay.

— 5 Arts and crafts representative —

How many people do you know who want to sell the products they make, using their skills in arts or crafts, but don't know how? Many of them lack good business sense and could do without the hassle of trying to sell their work. If only someone would act as their representative, they could focus on their work, while someone else made their sales.

What to offer

You will be offering your services as an arts and crafts representative or broker. You'll take artists' work to various shops, tourist destinations and other outlets and see if the owners or managers would like to stock them. Some hotels may be interested in having local theme paintings in the lobby and in guest rooms.

You will take the work to the weekly market and set up a stand to sell and display the work of the artists you represent. You will take commission on whatever you sell, at an agreed percentage of the selling price.

What you need

- artists to represent
- a supply of arts and crafts from the artists. Paintings should be complete with frames, provided by the artist.
- contacts with local giftshop and tourist shop owners
- business experience
- table, chair and umbrellas for weekly market
- a computer or an accounting ledger for keeping records of sales and your percentage from the sales
- transport
- a phone and a mobile phone or pager
- business cards, fliers and leaflets detailing your rates and services
- a diary
- a receipt book

Getting started

First, contact your friends who want their artwork and craftwork sold. Start out by representing them, and establishing your reputation as a broker. Then, you will be able to attract other artists. You may even 'discover' some unknown local talent with high artistic and money-making potential.

Once you have selected your clients and have samples of their work, start doing the rounds of the gift shops, tourist shops and the like. Book a stall for a local market. They will be the best outlet for your early sales. Keep abreast of arts and crafts fairs held in your region.

You should work out how to promote artists. A good starting point would be press releases to newsrooms, marked for the attention of specialist writers or the editor-in-chief. Apart from promoting individuals, you should also consider the news angle of local artists developing a thriving business and so on.

Contact local cafés and restaurants to ask if you can set up regular displays at their premises. This is an excellent way of showcasing talent and also adds character to the restaurant. Be sure to develop a mailing list of the art collectors and other establishments who buy from you, so you can keep them abreast of what's on offer and encourage 'repeat' business.

What to charge

It's customary to charge a percentage on the sales. I suggest a fee of ten to twenty per cent as a good starting rate. Don't forget, if you can't sell artwork after three or four weeks, talk to the artist or craftsperson, to discuss the marketability of their work.

6 Car boot sales

You may have noticed signs in your area promoting 'car boot sales' in almost any open spaces available at weekends. They are an excellent way to get rid of clothes and household items you don't want.

Car boot sales are normally promoted by means of posters and are often held on a regular date, like the first Sunday of each month. People can regularly set aside that date to visit the markets. Car boot sales are often organised by charities, so the fee may be in the form of a small donation. Check with the organisers regarding fees and their policies. Expect to pay anything in the range £5–20 to participate, and get there early for a good spot.

Car boot sales work like this. People arrive at their designated car park early in the morning, and are allocated a space. They park their car and then display their odds and ends and products in their car boot or on small tables.

It's an excellent way to sell your bric-a-brac, any arts and crafts you might make, or perhaps old clothes or even boots! The other benefit is that, unlike a garage sale where people come to you, the boot sale allows you to go where large crowds of people gather.

Here are a few tips for being successful.

- Arrive early. If you do, you'll get a good space and be ready for when the first customers arrive.
- Have a good range of items. Go through your cupboards and garage, and ask friends if they have items you can offer for sale. A variety of items will make your stand more interesting.
- Have bargain boxes. You could even put together bargain boxes or bargain bags of odds and ends. You might charge £5–10 per box, and they are easier to sell than individual items.

- Make sure you have a float of about £50 in change, and if the market is at the weekend, remember to go to the bank on Friday to organise the money. Keep the money in a bum bag, or in a secure cash tin.
- Take along plenty of recycled plastic or paper bags for customer purchases.
- Relax! Boot sales are meant to be fun, so enjoy yourself. Make sure you pack a picnic hamper so you don't get hungry.
- Be prepared to haggle or barter: people love to think they've saved a little money.
- Price items. It is also helpful if you mark larger items with price tags.

7 Garage sales

Garage sales are a great way to make money and get rid of unwanted goods. They are always held at the weekend. If you are planning one, start organising at least a week before the big day. Here are a few key steps to get you started.

Sort out what you want to sell

This sounds easier than it actually is. The whole family should go through their cupboards and boxes. Make sure you really want to sell the items you have chosen.

Sort items into categories

Set out five or six big boxes in a large room and sort all the clothes, shoes, records, electrical appliances and so on. This allows you to work out how much you'll be selling, what needs cleaning, washing etc.

Mark prices

You should mark all items with prices – use a washable felt-tip pen or stick-on labels.

Clear a space

Make sure you have a designated space to conduct your sale and make allowances for the weather. In case it rains, make sure you have shelter.

Advertise

Make sure your advertisement gets into the paper before the day of the sale. List the address, the time the sale starts and what's available (in category form).

You should also put up posters at shopping centres and on telephone poles in your area. Spread the word at work as well. The more who know, the more money you make.

On the day of the sale, put colourful signs with balloons or streamers at the major intersection near your house, at the end of your street and at the house itself.

Starting time

People always seem to ignore that – be prepared for the first knock on the door any time after 7.00 a.m.

Change and prices

Have at least £50 in change ready:

Also be prepared to haggle over prices – hardened garage-sale goers like nothing better than a good bargain.

Electrical appliances

No one expects you to give a guarantee, but make sure the appliance works and have a power point handy so people can try it themselves. Also have records, CDs or cassettes handy so people can test your music appliance.

Note: Selling electrical appliances can be fraught with danger, so check the regulations beforehand. In the UK, you should seek advice from the local trading standards office about the implications and responsibilities as far as safety is concerned.

Bargain boxes

Boxes containing a collection of items are a good way of selling the smaller pieces. You can call them 'bargain boxes': have a table full of items and allow people to choose, say, twenty items for £5–10.

Create a carnival atmosphere – you want to have fun and so do the garage-sale customers. Let your neighbours know about the sale beforehand and ask them if they have anything they might want to sell. Then perhaps you can promote it as a mammoth garage sale or a entire street sale.

Important fact

Remember your profit can only be tallied when you have subtracted the cost of advertising and preparation costs from your total day's earnings.

8 Selling firewood

On a cold winter's day there is nothing better than a roaring fire. But stop for a moment and think just where people are getting that firewood. If you live in the country or have access to woodland with trees that need lopping or felling this is a possible money-making scheme.

What to offer

You will be offering to supply people with trailer-loads of firewood, either chopped or unsplit (logs). You can also offer to sell people small bags of firewood.

What you need

- access to farmland needing clearing
- a van or a car and trailer
- a chain saw and an axe
- overalls, protective eye-wear, leather boots and gloves
- fridge magnets to remind people, when their stocks are running low
- a mobile phone or an answering machine
- business cards and leaflets detailing your rates and services
- a diary
- a receipt book
- a T-shirt advertising your business

Getting started

The most important question you should answer when setting up your business is where you are going to get the firewood to sell. If you own a farm you will have access to trees that need clearing, or fallen trees that can be cut up. If you don't, you can contact local farmers and offer to do some clearing for them, free of charge, or make a deal whereby you pay them a fee for allowing you to collect firewood from their property.

The best firewood comes from old fallen trees – it's dry, burns easily and is easy to collect.

Once you have a trailer-load ready, put an advertisement in the paper, and put posters up at shopping centres and stores that sell wood-burning stoves. You can also take your trailer-load to local markets and take orders. Most people like to buy their firewood by the trailer-load or by the bagful.

A good time to start advertising is just before the onset of winter – encourage people to think ahead.

What to charge

Set your rates either by the load or by the tonne. Find out what other wood-sellers are charging and set your fee accordingly. The fee will depend on how far you have to travel to get the wood, and the location of the client.

9 Selling manure

This money-making idea is one for someone with a strong stomach and a real 'nose' for business. Home owners love to spend money on fertiliser, hoses, garden equipment and garden plants. Fertiliser can be expensive and, as most garden experts will tell you, the best fertiliser is often the one from nature. So why not sell horse, sheep or chicken manure?

What to offer

You will be selling bags of 'nature's fertiliser', manure, for people to use in their gardens.

What you need

- a car and trailer to carry the manure
- a shovel for loading and bagging
- bags for the manure
- overalls
- wellington boots
- gloves
- a phone and a mobile phone or pager and an answering machine
- business cards, fliers and leaflets detailing your rates and services
- a diary
- a receipt book

Getting started

First ring local farms and stables. Many just dump their manure in big piles and do nothing with it, so find out which ones will let you collect the manure free of charge.

Arrange to go out once a week or once a fortnight and load up your trailer. Allow for up to 90 minutes of hard shovelling to fill the trailer. Then take the manure home and bag it. Hessian or thick plastic bags are probably best.

Next, advertise in the paper and put some posters up at local stores telling people you have manure for sale. It is best to advertise under the garden section.

Ring local garden groups and tell them about your service. Perhaps they have a newsletter you can advertise in. Local community groups might like to hear from you as well.

Contact local landscape gardeners and let them know you have manure for sale. They may be prepared to use your service or tell others about it. In return you might offer to hand out leaflets about the landscape service to your clients. This sort of arrangement benefits everyone. It's up to you whether you deliver or let people come to you.

People are more likely to use your service if you drop the manure off at their homes. It is easier and more convenient and gives you a line for your publicity: 'Mobile manure for your garden'.

What to charge

The best way to charge is by the bag. Work out how much it costs in petrol and your time to collect the manure, then set your prices. Also check local papers and visit local nurseries to find out how much they charge for manure. You can then set your prices competitively.

Start by asking £4–7 a bag or £15 for three bags. If people feel they are getting a bargain, they are likely to buy more.

10 Renting out your garage

Many people have a flat or house which is just too small. They often find that big, professional storage chains charge too much or are too far away. If you have an extra large garage, perhaps you should consider renting it out.

What to offer

You will be offering to store people's belongings in your garage.

What you need

- a garage or shed where people can store goods
- a phone
- a contractual agreement between yourself and the client
- insurance

Getting started

Check with estate agents in your area about the rules regarding renting out a garage. Next, you will need a basic rental contract which both you and the client sign. You should also have your garage insured.

When people rent out their garages they normally allow the person renting to padlock it and have it for their own use. This means you can no longer use your garage, much as if you were to rent out a flat on the top floor of your house. Most people advertise their garages for rent or storage in the local newspaper.

When I was in London, some friends decided to rent out their garage. They found a client by simply putting fliers on cars parked in the local area. Estate agents also handle the renting of garages but will expect a commission and a percentage of the rent.

What to charge

Check your local papers to see what other people are charging to rent out their garages. Then set either a weekly or monthly rental rate.

10

CREATING, MAKING AND MENDING

— 1 Making money from inventions —

Many of us have good ideas for inventions. It might be a simple household gadget or a complicated computer system which could be used by millions. But once you have that idea, how do you turn it into reality and into money?

According to the Inventors Association you should start by making a prototype of your invention. Then contact as many organisations or companies as possible that might use your product. You must find out if your invention is a viable product and what price people are willing to pay for it. You should also contact large companies that might be interested in mass-producing your invention.

Inventors need to work out the cost of producing their invention. If it can be made cheaply, it can be sold cheaply. Inventors can sometimes construct, package and market the product themselves, selling at wholesale prices to retail outlets. Market stalls are also a good place to try selling your invention.

It's important to give special consideration to patenting your invention. The more potential your invention has, the sooner it should be patented. If the prototype shows potential and there is market interest, you should consider patenting. However, inventions which are dangerous and are too much like other inventions may not be considered by the Patent Office.

For further information about patents contact the Patent Office.

2 Dial-a-dressmaker

I'm the sort of person who likes to modify current fashion and create my own dream outfits. But I just can't sew, so I take my ideas to a dressmaker who has the ability to work without patterns.

If you, too, possess this sort of ability, you have a marketable skill and should start cashing in.

What to offer

You will be offering to help men and women turn their fashion dreams into wearable reality. This will mean creating patterns, consulting on fabric choice and making the outfit.

What you need

- an ability to sew and work without patterns
- a sewing machine
- sewing supplies
- a workroom where you can set up your sewing machine, cut patterns and meet clients
- a portfolio with photos
- a phone or pager
- business cards, fliers and leaflets detailing your rates and services
- a diary
- a receipt book

Getting started

First, get together a series of photos of outfits you have completed. Dresses and outfits designed from scratch will spark the most interest from prospective clients. Then put an advertisement in the paper emphasising you can turn dreams into reality. Posters at fabric stores, shopping centres and formal hire outlets will also help attract attention.

Contact bridal boutiques and wedding coordinators and let them know the type of service you offer. You can offer a discount to clients they refer to you, so that they will be doing their clients a favour.

Consider contacting local shopping centres or social and sporting groups and offer to stage free fashion parades featuring your creations. You can then set up a stall, where you can hand out leaflets and talk to prospective clients. The idea is to tell as many people as you can about your skills.

What to charge

For small jobs, start at £10–20 an hour. For larger jobs, quote an overall figure using an hourly rate slightly less than your small-job rate.

--------- # 3 Large-size lingerie ---------

This is a great job for someone who is talented with the sewing machine and likes designing. My inspiration came from a woman in Australia. Karen Edbrooke was by her own admission big busted but she had a small waist. Her problem was she could never buy nice bras or lingerie in her larger size, so she made her own and now has over 2000 mail-order customers. Some of these women previously never went out of their houses because they have such large busts and couldn't buy bras. It was an untapped market.

What to offer

You will be making bras and lingerie for larger-size women and selling direct to lingerie stores or at the markets.

What you need

- sewing experience
- experience in making underwear; you can do adult education courses that teach this type of sewing
- a range of fabrics and designs
- cottons
- a phone and a mobile phone or pager
- business cards, fliers and leaflets detailing your rates and services

- a diary
- an order book
- a receipt book

Getting started

First do a course to bring yourself up to speed on working with the materials used to make bras and lingerie. Then design some simple bras, lace teddies and panties. Make them up in a range of fabrics and use lace to make them more appealing. Make your products luxurious and fun to wear. Larger-size women deserve the same respect that designers give to skinny girls.

Once you have a sample selection in a range of sizes, take them to your local lingerie stores and offer to supply them. Talk to your local shopping centre. Perhaps you could organise a fashion parade using larger-size women. You can also sell your products by organising Large Lingerie Parties. You could also set up a stand at the markets and have a photograph album of larger-size women posing in your designs.

Think of as many ways to get your message across as you can. This is almost an untapped market and if handled correctly could be a good earner.

What to charge

This will largely depend on the cost of your fabrics and the time taken to make the lingerie. Work out your costs and then add a profit margin of 30–50 per cent.

4 Mending clothes

This chore usually comes fairly low on the priority list in most households, despite the fact that in the long term it can save a lot of money. If you have a flair for sewing, you should consider this money-making scheme.

What to offer

You will be offering to repair people's clothes. It will include sewing on buttons, repairing rips and altering garments. This is of particular benefit for people who want last year's outfit to be given a makeover. Emphasise that point in your advertising – people will actually save money using your services.

It is best to offer a pick-up-and-return delivery service. All the client has to do is get together the clothes that need repairing.

What you need

- dressmaking skills
- cotton, thread, zips, needles etc.
- a reliable sewing machine
- transport
- a phone and a mobile phone or pager
- business cards, fliers and leaflets detailing your rates and services
- a diary
- a receipt book

Getting started

Placing an advertisement in the local paper is the best way to get the phone ringing. You could also ask local fabric shops if you can put up a poster and hand out fliers. Ask the fabric shop staff to recommend your service to clients. Have references and samples of your work on hand to show them.

Put up signs at local day nurseries and pre-school playgroups. Contact local government authorities in your area and ask if you can put up signs on their notice boards and advertise in their newsletters. Contact dry-cleaners and local laundromats. They may be willing to tell clients about your service or allow you to put up posters.

Consider letter-box drops and advertising in local school magazines. Parents are always looking for people to fix their children's uniforms.

What to charge

It is best to charge by the job. Find out what dry-cleaners charge for mending and set your rates just slightly lower. For example, if dry-cleaners charge £5 to replace a zip you should charge £4.50. Undercut their prices so you can develop a good client base. Once you are established, you can probably revise your costings upward.

——— 5 Fancy-dress making ———

If you have children you'll know fancy-dress parties are popular. It's fashionable to dress up as anything from fairies to fire eaters. However, many people have a good imagination but no sewing skill to put fancy dress ideas into practice. So, if you are one of those people who can sew up a storm, you should consider setting up a fancy-dress making service.

What to offer

You will be offering to make children's and adults' fancy-dress outfits for theme parties, birthday parties, and even school plays.

What you need

- an ability to sew
- experience making fancy dress outfits
- books on how to make a variety of fancy dress outfits
- an emergency box of fabrics, sequins, fairy wings, thread, braid, ribbon etc.
- a sewing machine
- a phone and a mobile phone or pager
- business cards, fliers and leaflets detailing your rates and services
- a diary to keep track of when the outfits are needed
- a receipt book

Getting started

Start by advertising in the local paper and perhaps, sending out a press release to the local media telling them about your unique service. You should also contact local schools, nursery schools and day nurseries. Let the managers know about your service. Put up posters and leave some fliers to be handed out to mums and dads. If the schools or centres have internal newsletters see if you can put ads in them about your service.

Visit local fabric shops and tell them about your service. Take along photos of costumes you have made so they can see your work first hand. Ask if you can put up posters or leave fliers for them to hand out. You will find your best advertisement will be by word of mouth.

What to charge

Consider charging £8–10 an hour, plus extra for any thread, fabric or other materials you have to provide. Give your clients an estimate as to how long the job will take. A skirt takes approximately two hours to make: wings take one hour. Alternatively you could charge per outfit.

6 Weaving hats

If you look on any street, at the races, a fete or at many holiday locations you are bound to see someone wearing a hat woven from raffia. At weekend markets they are big sellers. If this is an area which interests you, perhaps it's time you tried hat-making for profit.

What to offer

You will be making plaited straw and raffia hats and selling them at markets. You will also be offering to make these hats to order.

What you need

- completion of an adult education course in plaiting and making hats

- a supply of raffia and ribbons
- needles to sew plaits together
- leaflets about the care of raffia and straw hats
- a table, a chair and an umbrella for the market stall
- a phone and a mobile phone or pager
- business cards, fliers and leaflets detailing your rates and services
- a diary to keep track of orders
- a receipt book
- a T-shirt advertising your business

Getting started

First enrol in a hat-making course at your local adult education centre. Then make a selection of straw hats decorated with different
ribbons. Take the samples and set up a market stall. You can sell
what you have made and also take orders. You could also conduct hat-
making demonstrations to attract crowds and clients.

Another potential market could be local hotels and motels where
tourists stay – weekend hat-making displays and demonstrations
could lead to further sales.

What to charge

Most raffia hats start selling for around £15–40 depending on quality,
the hat-maker's experience and the decoration on the hat.

7 Celebration quilts

Marking a birthday, anniversary, graduation or special event with a
distinctive gift can be hard. The problem is finding just the right gift.
Celebration quilts are coming back into vogue. They are handmade
quilts or quilt covers which, through their design, mark a certain
event. Making and selling them can be quite lucrative for a talented
quilter.

What to offer

You will be offering to design and make special celebration quilts or quilt covers for birthdays and other special occasions.

What you need

- a talent for quilting and sewing
- an ability to design
- access to good-quality quilting materials
- a sewing machine, needles, thread and patterns
- a portfolio of quilts you have made, along with sample designs
- a phone and a mobile phone or pager
- business cards, fliers and leaflets detailing your rates and services
- a diary
- order and receipt books

Getting started

First, put together a portfolio of photographs of quilts you have made. You should also have a number of quilts on hand so people can examine the quality of your work. Draw up a few designs for typical quilts so clients will have plenty of ideas from which to choose.

The quilts should be decorated to reflect a personal aspect of the occasion. For instance, a wedding quilt could be made using the couple's favourite colours, or use a motif having personal significance. You might also embroider the couple's names, wedding date and the location where they were married.

A graduation quilt might show a silhouette of a graduate in cap and gown, or might show the university or college insignia. Again, you could embroider the name of the graduate, the degree or certificate awarded, the name of the college or university and the date.

Advertise your service in the paper. Also, ask the local fabric shop if you can put up posters and, perhaps, a special quilt display in the store. Offer to buy all the materials for your quilts from them in exchange for the quilt display, which will interest customers.

Encourage local gift shops to allow you to do the same.

Tell wedding organisers and caterers about your service and let stores selling toys and baby clothes know that you can make special 'birth quilts'. They will probably agree to let you put up a sign or posters. Maternity hospitals and baby health centres may also be prepared to display your flier.

Church groups, women's groups, nursery schools, child-care centres, sporting and other social groups could also be interested in hearing about your service.

What to charge

You should charge by the completed article. Here are some suggested prices.

- baby celebration quilt – £150
- teen celebration quilt – £200
- wedding quilt – £250

Much work goes into making the quilts so don't be afraid to ask these sorts of prices. Material costs can be included in the price or you can charge extra for them. Test the market, and adjust your prices accordingly.

8 Commemorative toys

Have you ever been to a reunion or a final class session and wished you had a keepsake from the occasion. Well, toys that can be signed or that have little signature books attached just might be the answer. They last longer than printed T-shirts or jumpers and can also be put on display.

What to offer

You will be offering to make commemoration toys for special events. They will either be a single, handmade toy for everyone at a party to sign, or a batch of manufactured toys you've decorated to be handed out to each person at a reunion. They can be made of plain calico, so that people can sign them, or they can have a signature book which hangs around the toy's neck or off its arm. Everyone in the class can sign them and remember the big day or event.

What you need

- an ability to sew and make toys
- material, stuffing etc. to make toys
- paper and card to make the autograph books
- business cards
- leaflets listing the type of toys you make and their prices
- transport
- a phone and a mobile phone or pager
- business cards, fliers and leaflets detailing your rates and services
- a diary
- an order book
- a receipt book

Getting started

First decide what types of toys you are going to offer and how you are going to make them. Then, make up a sample selection of celebration toys, some out of plain calico for people to sign directly and some with little signature books attached.

Next, contact local toy wholesalers and get quotations on various lots of 'naked' toys that you can dress – cuddly teddies or cute dolls. Have the information ready in advance of your customer orders.

To attract customers, you can advertise your service in the paper. Also set up a stall at a local market with your toys on display. Hundreds of people will see them and you can take orders.

Bridal boutiques, baby shops, formal hire shops, caterers and events managers are good sources of customers. Tell them about your service; ask if you can put up posters or if they will recommend you to clients.

Contact local schools, universities and other groups that may be organising reunions, formal events or other functions where your signature toys might be a big hit.

Get your message out to as many people as possible so they can help spread the word.

What to charge

The special one-off handmade toys will be the most expensive. Your price will depend on your time and effort and the materials required for that toy. You should be able to charge anything from £15 upwards for these 'boutique' toys.

The bulk toys will depend largely on their wholesale cost and your time spent in making their clothes and signature books. The client will expect a good deal or a volume discount on a large order.

9 Knitted toys

Home-made knitted toys are popular gifts and kids love them. If you are good at knitting this is a great business idea.

What to offer

You will be making knitted toys to sell at markets and to order.

What you need

- an ability to knit
- a receipt book and an order book
- knitting needles and yarn
- needles and thread
- buttons and toy eyes
- business cards
- a portfolio of photographs of toys you have made
- a table, chair and umbrella for the market stall
- a float of about £50 in change for market day
- a phone and a mobile phone or pager
- business cards, fliers and leaflets detailing your rates and services
- a diary
- a receipt book
- a T-shirt or sweatshirt advertising your business

Getting started

First, knit some stock toys. Compile a display album (a photo album will do) of toys you can make to order. On each of the photographs, be sure to put the price and time required to make the toy. Put together a selection of toys to sell on a market stall. Then book a stall at your local market.

You could arrange to visit playgroups and nursery school meetings to show parents your selection of toys. This is a good captive market where you can take orders. People who live in retirement villages may also like to see your toys for gifts. Contact local gift and tourist stores to ask if they would like to stock your products.

What to charge

Take into consideration the cost of the yarn and your time, when setting a price on the toys. Small toys should be priced at about £5–10. Remember you are offering high-quality handmade toys.

10 Antique restorer

Thousands of people have old pieces of furniture they have put aside to restore one day. They promise themselves they will make time, but usually the chair or table just ends up in the corner gathering dust. If you are good with sandpaper and varnish, setting up a mobile restoring business may just be the way for you to make money.

What to offer

You will be offering to come to people's homes to strip or sand tables, chairs and other furniture so they can complete the restoration themselves. The alternative service is to completely restore their old furniture.

What you need

- experience in restoring furniture

- sandpaper, wire brushes and an electric sander
- a selection of varnishes
- a hammer, chisels, screwdrivers and other tools
- overalls and other protective clothing
- a portfolio showing photographs of pieces you have completed
- transport
- fridge magnets
- a phone and a mobile phone or pager
- business cards, fliers and leaflets detailing your rates and services
- a diary
- a receipt book

Getting started

The first step is to make sure your restoration skills are up to scratch. You might consider doing an antique restoration course which will also add credibility to you as a business person.

Once that is completed let people know exactly what kind of service you offer – that is, the option of a complete restoration or just stripping and sanding. Advertise your service in local papers, by letter-box dropping in your neighbourhood and by handing out fliers and business cards at antique auctions and fairs. Ask paint and hardware shops if they will let you put up posters and leave business cards. You should then offer people a discount if they hear about your service from the shop.

Use your portfolio to best effect. Have it ready to show people what you can do. Offer them free quotations. When you do a quotation be sure to give them a thorough breakdown of all costs involved.

What to charge

Your price will depend on the size of the job. The aim of your service is to make it affordable. For small jobs, charge by the hour, but for larger jobs lower your hourly rate and quote a daily rate. Your hourly rate should start around £10–20. Your daily rate should start at around £100.

—— 11 Recycled mirror making ——

Furniture that has a rustic feel is very fashionable. If you are good with wood then consider making mirrors with recycled frames.

What to offer

You will be making recycled mirrors using second-hand wood from demolished buildings, old farms or wood which offers unusual texture. You will sell the mirrors at local markets.

What you need

- experience in woodworking
- a supply of second-hand wood off-cuts – old floor boards, fence palings, anything that offers character or a 'lived in' feel
- nails, saws, wood glue
- a supply of mirrors cut to the shapes of your wooden frames
- glass-cutting tools
- a range of designs for your mirrors, large and small, rectangular, square, oval etc.
- a portfolio showing photographs of mirrors you have made
- a market stall
- a phone and a mobile phone or pager
- business cards, fliers and leaflets
- a diary
- order and receipt books
- a T-shirt or sweatshirt advertising your business

Getting started

First find your wood – it has to offer character and maybe tell a story. Wood from old floorboards or farm fences is great. Frames need to be strong and well jointed, even though they are made from recycled wood. It may be easier to match the frame to the shape of the mirror, rather than cut the mirror to fit a frame, at least until you are more experienced. When you have finished the frame, sand it until it is smooth and then stain or paint it before fitting the mirror.

Once you have a selection of mirrors, set up your market stall. Have your portfolio on hand to show people what you can do and be prepared to take special orders for weddings or birthdays.

These mirrors are different from those bought in shops as they are slightly rustic and offer rural charm – and best of all they are recycled.

What to charge

This largely depends on what your wood and mirror costs. The wood should be reasonably cheap if purchased from second-hand stores. You should charge according to the size and the amount of work which went into the mirror. Add on 30–40 per cent profit for yourself.

——— 12 Designer invitations ———

If you have organised a wedding recently, you'll know the importance of being different or distinctive. So, if you are a talented craftsperson and are good at calligraphy you should consider cashing in by offering to make unusual wedding invitations. Of course, you can offer the same service for other celebrations such as christenings or anniversaries.

What to offer

You will be offering handmade wedding invitations that are unique, with that extra 'something' that will make guests remember the happy day.

What you need

- imagination
- experience as an artist or craftsperson
- good handwriting and calligraphy skills
- samples of invitations you can make and samples of your ideas
- references from satisfied customers
- a phone, answering machine, mobile phone or pager

- business cards, fliers and leaflets detailing your rates and services – make sure they are unusual, to reflect your talent
- a diary
- a receipt book
- a T-shirt advertising your business

Getting started

Get some basic craft books that show you how to make invitations. If you are not experienced in calligraphy, why not do an adult education course? Talk to friends who have recently got married to find out what their invitations were like, and what they really would have preferred. Talk to managers of wedding stores and find out what the current trends are and what young brides and grooms are requesting.

For a service like this to stand any chance of success, you need to be unique. Unusual wedding invitations include an invitation posted in a bottle, an invitation crumpled up and delivered in a pretty box, invitations made on recycled paper, invitations done up in scroll form, invitations printed on pretty scarves or lengths of silk, and invitations printed on T-shirts (the invitation you can wear).

Make up some samples and then advertise your service in the newspaper. Contact wedding organisers in your town or city and arrange a meeting. Show them your samples and ask if they might be able to use you. Contact wedding shops and tell them about your service. You might also consider advertising in bridal magazines. Contact popular reception venues and tell the managers about your service. Show them your samples and ask if you can leave them some fliers to hand out.

Find out when the next craft fair will be in your local community. Arrange to have a stand, either by yourself or with a group of people who provide wedding services.

What to charge

Keep a list of all costs involved in making the invitations. Remember to charge for your time and add a profit margin of 20–50 per cent on top of this, then divide by the number of invitations you have made so that you can quote 'per invitation'.

Make sure you provide a thorough breakdown of costs in any quotation.

_____ 13 Handmade paper and _____ greetings cards

Handmade paper and greetings cards are currently in vogue. They are part of the recycling trend we are seeing at present and are a very personal way of sending a message to someone.

What to offer

You will be making up sets of handmade note-paper, notelets and envelopes for sale at markets. You will also be using your handmade paper to make greeting cards decorated with glitter, sparkles, buttons and other unusual products. You will sell your products at markets and offer to take orders – perhaps designing cards and note-paper to suit your individual clients.

What you need

- a paper-making kit (available from craft shops)
- newspaper and other used paper for making recycled paper
- glitter, sparkles and other decorations for cards
- glue
- cellophane and ribbon to wrap up the sets
- a table, chair and umbrella for market stall
- a phone and a mobile phone or pager
- business cards (made from your handmade paper!), fliers and leaflets detailing rates for your personally designed cards and paper
- a diary to keep track of orders
- a receipt book
- a T-shirt or sweatshirt advertising your business

Getting started

First, make a selection of note-paper, notelets and envelopes using your handmade paper kit. Decorate them as interestingly as possible – each should have its own individual style. The sets should contain ten notelets or twelve pieces of note-paper, and ten envelopes. Use cellophane and ribbon to package the sets and don't forget to include your business card.

Next, take your samples to the markets. Have on hand your portfolio of samples of different styles you can produce. Take your samples to gift and tourist shops in the area and see if they are willing to stock your product. Wedding invitations produced on recycled paper are quite popular so contact the local bridal wear shop and ask to leave some fliers.

What to charge

Your prices will depend largely on how long it takes you to make and package the sets. Start off at around £5–10 per set. You can sell individual cards with envelopes for around £1–3 each. If you take orders requiring a special theme or style, you can charge a little more. Don't forget to offer group and quantity discounts.

—— 14 Decorating plant-pots ——

We have all seen terracotta pots for plants. They serve their purpose, but they are quite plain. So, if you have some artistic ability, why not decorate the pots and saucers and sell them at markets as designer pots?

What to offer

You will be hand-decorating terracotta pots with paint and dried flowers. You will be selling them at markets and directly to nurseries and gift stores.

What you need

- artistic ability
- a supply of terracotta pots (Try to buy them direct from the distributors, at wholesale prices. You'll need a selection of sizes.)
- paints that won't wash off when the pots get wet
- varnish
- a supply of brushes and paint cleaners
- stencil designs from craft stores
- craft wire
- dried flowers
- craft glue
- transport
- a phone and a mobile phone or pager
- business cards, fliers and leaflets detailing your rates and services
- a diary
- a receipt book

Getting started

First purchase a selection of pots, then start decorating. To decorate a pot, simply paint it, using a selection of colours.

Paint the top rim one colour, the bottom section a different colour and cover with a varnish. If you feel adventurous, use stencils from craft shops to decorate the pots in a more intricate fashion.

If you'd rather decorate your pot with dried flowers, start by gluing a selection of flowers to the top five centimetres of the pot to create a crown. After gluing, spray the flowers with hair lacquer to prevent them from breaking. You can weave ribbon in among the flowers or attach small animal figurines bought from a craft store.

Once you have a good selection, take some photos for your portfolio, then take the pots to the markets. Take some samples to plant nurseries and gift stores. Another good way of generating business is to ask local cafés or restaurants if they will allow you to set up a pot display for a few weeks. Don't forget to attach your business card to each pot so people know who they can contact to place orders.

What to charge

Your price will depend on your costs for pots, materials and time. Remember, these pots are 'designer originals' and you should promote that element to potential clients.

15 Table and menu-board decorator

Café society is becoming widespread. Little cafés and delicatessens are opening up everywhere, selling coffee and snacks. Competition for customers is tough, and one way of attracting them is by having unusually painted tables and chalkboard menus.

What to offer

You will be offering to paint the café tables in wild and exotic colours. You will also make weekly visits to do up their menu chalkboard in vivid colours, with hand-drawn pictures and designs.

What you need

- artistic flair
- a collection of high-quality chalks (many professionals use 'liquid' chalks)
- a collection of high-quality paints and brushes
- a basket or case for your paints and chalks
- a portfolio of photographs showing your work
- a few small second-hand tables, to decorate and photograph for the portfolio
- a few chalkboards for sample menus, to be photographed for the portfolio
- transport
- a phone and a mobile phone or pager
- business cards, fliers and leaflets detailing your rates and services
- a diary
- a receipt book
- overalls or a T-shirt advertising your business

Getting started

First, put together a portfolio of your ideas. Do up a number of chalkboard menus at home and take photos of them. Paint a number of tables – decorate them with flowers, birds or other designs.

Then start the foot-slogging. Visit as many cafés and restaurants as possible to tell them about your service. Perhaps you could offer to do the first menu board free or at a discount.

Try selling your decorated tables at the markets and at local furniture shops. The more unusual and arty they are, the more likely they are to sell.

What to charge

Chalkboards

Charge according to the size of the boards and amount of artwork required. Aim for an hourly rate of around £15–30.

Tables

Charge according to the size and the artwork required. Again set an hourly rate.

—— 16 Designer sling-maker ——

If you have ever broken your arm or wrist and been given a rather boring grey or white sling you will understand why this is a great money-making scheme. Recovering from an injury can often be made harder if the bandages and slings are awful colours. So if you are good with a sewing machine consider this option.

What to offer

You will be making arm and wrist slings in a range of materials, some in bright colours, others using bright, modern prints.

What you need

- sewing skills and a sewing machine
- a range of bright materials and decorations
- basic design of an arm sling and wrist sling
- a phone and a mobile phone, pager or answer machine
- business cards, fliers and leaflets detailing your rates and services
- a diary or order book
- a receipt book

Getting started

The first thing you should do is buy a wrist sling and an arm sling. Study how they are made and then design a template for your slings. Make up a batch of arm and wrist slings, using bright materials – the brighter and more interesting, the better. The aim of these slings is for the wearer to make a fashion statement while recuperating, and to match their sling with the clothes they wear.

You could also consider using stretch fabric to make a cover for a plaster leg cast. It should fit over the cast – a bit like a sock but with both ends cut off.

Once you have a range made up take them to the local hospital shop, to local doctors and local pharmacies, physiotherapists and anywhere that might sell slings. Perhaps the local ambulance service may be interested. Rehabilitation centres, especially for children, are also a good place to sell your wares – kids love bright colours and this way their sling can be a real talking point.

Make sure you leave your card and fliers and even a few samples of your work. Then – hopefully – the orders will start to come in. You should also consider a press release, not only to your local paper but also to medical magazines read by nurses and doctors.

What to charge

This will depend on the type of materials you use. A basic arm sling should start at around £10 and a wrist sling should be a little less. Charge more if the product is decorated.

17 Designer bird and squirrel boxes

Birds – and sometimes squirrels – can make themselves at home in the roofs of houses. They choose to live inside roofs because, with urban sprawl, their natural habitat is in increasingly short supply. Providing a 'designer' box to lure them out can solve the problem and give the client's garden a special touch.

What to offer

You will be making nesting boxes for birds and squirrels out of recycled timber, old roofing materials and branches from lopped trees. The rustic charm and soundness of recycled materials will help sales. The boxes can also be painted the same colour as the house to add a special element.

What you need

- old pieces of timber
- roofing felt or straw for a thatched roof
- branches about 3 centimetres in diameter
- nails
- a hammer
- an electric saw
- paint and brushes
- a telephone answering machine, or a mobile phone or pager
- business cards and leaflets detailing your rates and services
- a diary
- a receipt book
- a T-shirt advertising your business

Getting started

Bird and squirrel boxes are easy to make. Simply nail four pieces of wood together to form the base, back and sides in a basic box shape, then complete the little house with a waterproof roof. Make the front section with a hole for the animals to get in and out, and cut a smaller hole below that to rig up a perch made of a stick or doweling.

Once this is done, paint the box in common house colours. Boxes painted to match the home's colour scheme will be especially popular. To add some character, buy stencils from the craft shop, or if you have artistic flair, paint on some motifs such as flowers, or even windows.

After you have made a few boxes of various sizes, shapes and colours you can give some thought to your selling and marketing strategy. Markets are a good place to start. You can get a stand for around £20–30 a day. Alternatively, visit nurseries, gift stores and garden and hardware shops. See if they are interested in stocking your product.

Advertise in the local paper. Don't forget, send out a press release to the local media. They may love a squirrel box story, especially if you have something cute in the box, for a photo.

What to charge

You should charge £15–40 for a box. The exact price will depend on how big it is. When working out your price take into account the cost of your wood, nails, iron, paint and time.

—— 18 Dial-a-bike repair service ——

Cycling is growing in popularity in many countries. In large cities like London there are many cycling couriers and in Europe off-road cycling and bike-racing is hugely popular.

If you are skilled at bike repairs, puncture repairs or push-bike servicing, consider setting up a mobile repair service.

What to offer

You will be offering to service and repair people's push-bikes and punctures at their home, at the office or on the road in an emergency situation. These days, many people ride their bikes to work. With their busy schedules, they would appreciate using your service.

What you need

- a knowledge of bike repair, puncture repair and bike servicing
- business cards, leaflets and posters
- a good supply of bike parts and a puncture repair kit
- contacts with local suppliers for bike parts
- transport
- a phone and a mobile phone or pager
- business cards, fliers and leaflets detailing your rates and services
- a diary
- a receipt book
- a T-shirt advertising your business

Getting started

This is a specialist service, so consider advertising in bike magazines as well as in the local paper. Contact local bike clubs (both social and sporting groups) and tell them about your service. Don't forget to offer discounts. Put up colourful posters on bike path notice boards and along the bike path itself. Also contact local schools and universities to ask if you can advertise in their newsletters or put up posters.

A quick check of the bicycle racks at local office parking areas will give you an idea of the number of people there who ride bikes to work. If there are sufficient to make it worthwhile, put posters up in common areas and do a leaflet drop. Put your leaflets on the push-bikes to get your message directly to the users.

What to charge

This will depend largely on how far you have to travel and the extent of repair required. Try setting a flat rate for bike servicing, with parts charged separately. Here are some suggested fees.

- puncture repair – £5 flat rate plus parts
- bike service – £10–20 flat rate plus parts
- bike repair – £10–20 per hour plus parts

Be sure to charge a premium for an emergency road service.

19 Face-painting

Kids love to have their faces painted. With some non-toxic paint and a few deft strokes of the brush, they are transformed into their favourite character. If you have an artistic bent and are good with kids and large groups, setting up a face-painting service could be a lot of fun.

What to offer

You will offer to go to birthday parties, anniversaries and other celebrations to paint guests' faces. You will also offer to be a special guest at pre-school and day nurseries painting the kids' faces. You can also set up a stall at shopping centres and malls as a face painter/entertainer (remember you will need a permit). You might consider setting up outside big sporting events such as football and soccer matches and offering to paint supporters' faces as they go in.

What you need

- artistic flair
- a face-painting kit and brushes
- a plastic apron for you
- funny little toys attached to your apron to keep big and little kids amused
- portable chairs and table
- a mirror for clients to see their faces
- a portfolio of photos of satisfied customers
- a Polaroid camera (Clients may want a photograph of the end result.)
- permission from the local council, mall operators and local business associations
- transport
- a phone and a mobile phone or pager
- business cards, fliers and leaflets detailing your rates and services
- a diary
- a receipt book
- a T-shirt advertising your business (or have the apron specially printed)

Getting started

First, put together your portfolio of photographs of faces you have painted, to show to clients. Then advertise in the paper. Put posters up at toy stores and kids' clothing shops, at party-goods supply shops, at places where toddlers' groups meet, at nursery schools, day nurseries and at fancy-dress shops.

Visit local childminding centres, tell them about your service and find out if they want to hire you for a day. Do the same with local schools – they might have fetes or school plays that may require your services – although they may want very special rates or a percentage of your takings.

Contact parents' groups and playgroups, and let them know about your service. Competition for good entertainers for kids' parties is high, as all mums and dads want their little ones to have the best.

Also contact local theatre and drama groups. They may want to employ you for their plays.

Visit local shopping centre managers, show them your portfolio and see if they will let you work in their mall, particularly during school holidays. Then, get any necessary approvals.

Visit local leisure and sports centres. Try the places where sports clubs meet (such as football grounds) and get the approval of their managers to set up outside the big weekend games to decorate supporters. You could also try offering your services from a stall at the local market.

What to charge

Charge per face for most jobs. Start at £2.50 for a simple face and push it up to about £5 for a more complicated face. If you are visiting a pre-school playgroup, quote a group rate, say £30 for an hour and you'll do as many faces as possible. In shopping centres you can either quote a day rate or charge per face in a 'busking' set-up.

—— 20 Street-theatre busking ——

Thousands of people enjoy watching buskers, but what if you don't feel your musical skills are up to it? Don't throw the idea away, because singing buskers no longer rule the roost. Street theatre attracts large crowds these days. If you're good at acting, perhaps it's something you should consider.

What to offer

You will be working as a street-theatre busker at malls and shopping centres on the weekends and during holiday periods.

What you need

- a talent for acting
- a good series of street theatre acts
- costumes
- free time on weekends and holidays to busk
- permission from local business associations, local council and mall operators
- a container for the money paid by shoppers
- colourful posters telling shoppers about your performance

Getting started

First work out a series of acts that will entertain shoppers. Street theatre is about acting, entertaining antics and involving members of the crowd. Remember, when you busk it's the people who gather around you who want to see and hear your act – do not harass shoppers who are merely walking by. Once you have an act you are happy with, develop a colourful costume.

Find out what approval you need to busk. Many local authorities and local business associations require buskers to be registered and licensed. Talk to buskers in your area, and contact your local authority to find out what is required of you. Once you get approval, you can start performing.

When doing a street-theatre performance you should work the crowd – involve people. Keep each performance to around 10–15 minutes, but if the crowd tell you they want more, give it to them. Popular street theatre ideas include:

- the dinner-suited masked figure who appears statue-like but changes position when shoppers are not looking
- mime artists
- tumblers
- a team of actors who perform short plays for children
- actors who cover themselves in tubes made of wire and lycra and take on crazy, worm-like shapes

What to charge

What you make will depend on what the shoppers give you. If you're good and attract a large crowd, you can make £30–60 an hour during peak times. Remember to keep an eye on your money as there are some who find buskers an easy target for theft.

11

ARE YOU GREEN AT HEART?

1 Dial a 'green' consultant

We all want to do our bit to make the world 'greener', but sometimes it is difficult to know where to start. I, for one, should like to know just what I can do in my daily life to be 'greener'. I should like to know if my home or office is environmentally friendly. If you are environmentally aware, and have a 'pro-green' lifestyle, why not make money by sharing your knowledge with others?

What to offer

You will be offering to come into clients' homes or offices to advise on 'green' improvements they can make. You'll provide them with information on how they can live in a 'greener' way. You'll also suggest lifestyle changes and even modifications to individual rooms that will help save the planet.

What you need

- a commitment to environmental causes
- some experience and a 'green' lifestyle
- pamphlets on how to live 'greener' to give to clients
- 'green diaries' for clients to record their lifestyle changes
- good contacts and membership of local environmental groups

- a portfolio of testimonials
- transport
- a phone and a mobile phone or pager
- business cards, fliers and leaflets detailing your rates and services
- a diary
- a receipt book
- a T-shirt advertising your business

Getting started

First, contact local 'green' groups and do as much research as possible about living 'green'. You need to become an expert. Compile a list of 'green' tips for home or office, including grocery shopping and lifestyle recommendations. Next, try out your consulting skills on friends and neighbours before launching your business.

Once you have completed your research, put the information in booklet form. Have the booklets photocopied and spiral bound at a local printer. Then start advertising in the local paper, in local newsletters and in magazines. Contact 'green' groups and ask them if they will recommend you to their members. They may also have newsletters in which you can advertise. Offer discounts to those members who use your service.

Contact associations for asthma and allergy sufferers, as well as other groups concerned with environmentally induced illness. Hand out fliers at their meetings and, if possible, advertise in their newsletters.

Try contacting local builders and interior decorators. They may consider recommending you to their clients. Also contact local businesses: you can offer to come in and set up recycling stations and implement other 'green' office ideas.

Consider doing local letter-box drops and putting fliers under windscreen wipers in large car parks. The more people who know about your service, the more who will use it.

What to charge

You should charge by the visit. For example:

- a home visit – £20
- a complete 'green' overhaul for the office – £60

Offer follow-up visits and lists of stores where people can buy 'green-friendly' products to continue on their road to 'green' success.

—— # 2 Green-friendly repellents ——

The concern about chemicals in cleaning products and in insect repellents is growing almost daily. Many people are allergic to the toxic substances used, and parents of small children are concerned about the long-term effects of the products. Consequently, the market for 'green' repellents and cleaners is growing, and old herbal remedies are making a comeback.

What to offer

You will be making up herbal repellents in bottles or in trigger-action spray containers. You will also be growing herbs in pots to use to repel mosquitoes and other biting insects. You will sell all these products on a stall at weekend markets.

What you need

- a selection of dried lavender, spearmint, wormwood, basil, thyme and lemon grass
- a selection of essential oils (use the list of dried herbs)
- aloe vera
- olive or grapeseed oil
- herb books
- recycled glass or plastic bottles and trigger-action spray containers
- information leaflets
- table, chair and umbrella for the market
- labels with date of manufacture, use-by date and instructions
- a phone and a mobile phone or pager
- business cards, fliers and leaflets detailing your rates and services
- a diary
- order and receipt books
- a T-shirt or sweatshirt advertising your business

Getting started

First, research herbal remedies for natural repellents at your local library. Contact environmental groups that may have information about herbal remedies. Then, try the remedies out for yourself. Here are some ideas to get you started.

- Make a repellent using lavender to deter mosquitoes. Use aloe vera as a base and add some dry lavender. You could add a few drops of lavender essential oil. People can put the solution in a trigger-action spray container to repel the insect pests.
- Make a mixture of borax and sugar, to get rid of ants or silverfish. People can rub some on skirting boards and other problem areas to rid their house of the pests.
- Grow insect-repelling plants in small pots. Eau de cologne and the flowers of mint and pyrethrum plants keep away flying insects.

If you present these insect-repellent solutions in attractive containers and marketable packages, you can sell them at markets. With each bottle, include an instruction leaflet explaining how to use the solution.

Don't forget a warning label on all products you sell – although they may be environmentally friendly, they may be toxic if eaten or drunk. Include a warning about keeping products away from children.

Important fact

Check with your local authority or council health department for any special legislation governing sale of these products. You may be required to obtain a special permit.

What to charge

Your prices should be competitive with chemical options being sold at the supermarket. Try charging a little less so people are encouraged to try the green alternative. A 500 ml (16 fl oz) bottle of mosquito deterrent could be sold for around £4.

When setting your prices make sure you take into account all your raw materials cost and add a decent profit for yourself. Start with a mark-up of 30–40 per cent. If you find that people are prepared to pay more, then increase your prices accordingly.

—— 3 Organic shopping service ——

A common theme running through this book is that people have very little time on their hands. Given that people have also become increasingly health-conscious, there is a clear need for an organic or 'green' shopping service. Finding shops that sell 'organic' products is often difficult and can mean a lot of running around. If you are willing to do the required research which defeats many potential shoppers, your service just may be a winner.

What to offer

You would be buying clients' weekly fruit and vegetables as well as cleaning products. But, instead of just going to the supermarket, you would be buying only organic and chemical-free products.

Because you would be supplying all your clients' organic products, including soaps and cleansers, you would be providing more than just the fruit and vegetables offered by most organic delivery services.

The clients would phone in their orders and you would buy and deliver their 'green' requests.

What you need

- a list of all wholesale and retail outlets that sell organic and environmentally friendly produce: that includes sellers of fruit and vegetables, bread, flour and cleaning products
- a car, for pick-up and delivery
- a phone and a mobile phone or pager
- business cards, fliers and leaflets detailing your rates and services
- a diary, to keep track of appointments
- a receipt book
- a T-shirt advertising your business

Getting started

The first problem is to find out where you can buy these 'green' products. Start by looking up health-food stores and organic suppliers in the phone book. Prepare lists of products and produce and their prices, for people to refer to when placing their orders. Next, advertise your service in the newspaper. Remember to send out press releases to the local media – this sort of service is wacky enough to get attention.

Visit local delicatessens, restaurants, cafés and hotels to see if they are interested in buying organic products. Leave leaflets at nursery schools and after-school care centres: parents want their children to have the best – and these days the best is organic.

Contact professional groups in your town or area and tell them about your service. People who work long hours and also want quality products would be among your better customers.

Another way to attract attention is to leave a poster and leaflets at the local gym: fit people are usually interested in high-quality and healthful food.

What to charge

You will need to charge a shopping and delivery fee. The fee will depend on how far you have to travel and how many clients you buy for at one time. Start at around £5–8 per delivery. Take receipt of payment upon delivery.

———— 4 Green cleaning ————

These days many people use house-cleaners as they find changing work patterns give them less time at home. Now if you combine that need with the increasing need for 'green' awareness you will realise there is a growing market for house-cleaning, using only environmentally friendly products.

What to offer

You will be offering to come to people's homes to clean with 'green' products or 'green' methods. This is especially good for people who suffer asthma, allergies or chronic fatigue syndrome.

What you need

- a commitment to 'green' causes
- a knowledge of 'clean green' methods
- 'green' cleaning products
- gloves, rags and scrubbing brushes
- fridge magnets
- a phone and a mobile phone or pager
- business cards, fliers and leaflets detailing your rates and services
- a diary
- a receipt book
- a T-shirt advertising your business

Getting started

First, research and find out from environmental groups what types of products and methods are considered 'green' and environmentally safe. You should also become a member of these groups if you have the sort of commitment to set up a business like this. Here are some 'green-friendly' cleaning methods.

- Windows can be cleaned using newspapers and a mixture of vinegar and water.
- Bathrooms can be cleaned using a scrubbing brush and bicarbonate of soda.
- Eucalyptus oil or tea-tree oil can be used to disinfect cleaned areas.
- Vinegar also makes a great grease cutter.

Once you have worked out your 'clean green' methods you can advertise in local papers, and put up posters at shopping centres and health-food stores. You should also leave posters and leaflets with asthma, allergy and other health associations, as chemicals and cleaning fluids can cause allergic reactions.

What to charge

You should charge by the hour. Going rates should start at around £8–10 an hour, with home-owners providing their own products. Check the rates charged by ordinary house-cleaners. You should be able to charge more because you are a 'designer cleaner' – cleaning the 'green' way takes more muscle and is a special service.

5 Environmentally friendly oven cleaning

Have you noticed that cleaning the oven is the job that most people hate more than almost any other? But every house has at least one oven and, with the popularity of microwave ovens, probably two. If you can take on this messy, time-consuming, undesirable but essential job, you could cash in.

Some large cleaning firms do offer oven cleaning, but the cost can be prohibitive or it may be done as part of a larger, more expensive deal that might include cleaning the carpets and curtains. A personalised oven-cleaning service using environmentally friendly products is likely to be a hit, especially with the elderly, with those who work full-time, and with people who suffer from asthma and other respiratory problems. For them, cleaning an oven is almost impossible because of the fumes given off by cleaning fluids.

What to offer

The service you will offer is personalised oven cleaning. It will be a thorough job, to include hobs and microwave ovens. You can also offer to clean people's barbecues.

What you need

- wire brushes and scrubbing brushes
- scrapers to get rid of the grime
- face mask
- rubber gloves
- cleaner (You can either use commercial oven cleaners from supermarkets or try citrus-based, non-toxic cleaners you can get from health food and green stores. These do just as good a job and don't leave nasty fumes.)
- a phone and a mobile phone or pager
- business cards, fliers and leaflets detailing your rates and services
- a diary
- a receipt book
- a T-shirt or plastic apron with your business name printed on it

Getting started

Advertise in your local paper, stress the environmentally friendly aspect of your service. Posters at local shopping centres and letterbox drops will also help drum up business. Tell local senior citizens' groups about the service as well as other community groups. You could also try setting up a small information stall at a local market to promote your service and take bookings.

If you are using 'green' products, ask your local health store if you can put up a poster.

What to charge

This will depend on how far you travel to the job and the cleaners you use. Try setting your prices at around £10 for a full oven clean, and £5 for hobs.

12

GOOD IN THE GARDEN?

1 Growing seedlings

Gardens and indoor plants are never out of fashion, so growing seedlings and pot plants could become a lucrative business venture for you.

What to offer

You will be growing seedlings and selling pot plants. You will sell home-grown plants at local markets. This is also a great opportunity to get together with friends to form a plant-growing co-operative.

What you need

- green fingers
- easy-to-grow seeds
- old yoghurt containers, milk cartons and juice boxes with the tops cut off and holes punched in the bottoms, for raising seedlings
- a supply of pots
- access to good soil or seedling mixture
- compost (make your own and save money)
- a card table, for your market stall
- a float of about £50 in change for your market day
- a phone and a mobile phone or pager

- business cards, fliers and leaflets detailing your rates and services
- a diary
- a receipt book

Getting started

First raise some seedlings. Check with your local garden shop to see what is currently in season. The best sellers are vegetable seedlings. Flowering plants are always popular, especially hardy ones requiring little tending. Herbs also sell quickly.

Cultivate the seedlings in the yoghurt containers, cut-off milk cartons or any other recycled pots you can find. The combination of 'green awareness' and recycling is a very positive marketing image.

Look around your garden for plants that will grow from cuttings. When they 'take', you can sell them as well. Some plants that are easy to grow include:

- Madonna lily *Lilium candidum*
- Ornamental figs *Ficus*
- Nodding violet *Streptocarpus*
- Geranium *Pelargonium*
- Happy plants *Pracaena*
- Philodendron *Philodendron*
- Basil *Ocimum basilicum*
- Chives *Allium schoenoprasum*
- Parsley *Petroselinum crispum*
- Capsicum *Capsicum frutescens*
- Beans *Phaseolus*
- Corn *Zea mays*
- Pumpkin *Curcurbita*
- Tomato *Lycopersicon esculentum*

Once you have a supply of seedlings and plants, contact your local market. Find out the fee for a stall: most markets charge £20–30 for a stall per day. You should arrive early, around 7 a.m., with a supply of food and drink to keep you fortified. Why not get a stall together with a friend? The more plants you have the better.

What to charge

Visit as many markets as possible to find out how much plants are selling for. This is the best guide for determining market prices. Don't undervalue your product, and make sure you cover your costs, especially the rental of the stall for the day. Start by charging around £2–3 for a tray of vegetable or flower seedlings and £3 or more for pot plants.

2 Selling herbs

Recent years have seen a big boom in the popularity of Asian, Italian and nouvelle cuisine – which all require fresh herbs. If you are smart, you can take advantage of the trend, and you don't have to be a chef!

What to offer

You will be supplying herbs to local restaurants and delicatessens, and selling them at local markets. The herbs will be grown organically and will be free of pesticides and herbicides.

Getting started

Grow a few sample herbs and take them to local restaurants to see if they are interested in buying. You'll probably be surprised by the reaction – healthy fresh herbs are often hard to come by. Consider growing herbs in individual containers. When they're mature, you can sell them at the local market, ready for people to transplant into their own gardens or use in that evening's dinner.

Another outlet to sell your herbs is through local greengrocers and supermarkets. They may be interested in buying your herbs at wholesale prices for resale in their vegetable section.

What you need

To grow herbs at home, you need an area of the garden with good-quality soil. If you are going to sell the herbs in a ready-to-transplant form, grow them in individual containers with holes punched in the base. Recycled yoghurt containers, fruit drink or milk cartons will work just fine. Herbs in demand at restaurants and at markets include:

- basil
- chives
- chervil
- tarragon
- coriander
- parsley
- oregano.

What to charge

If you are selling herb plants in containers at markets, you'll probably be able to ask £1–3 per container, depending on the plants' age and condition.

Selling to restaurants is a different matter. To set prices, go to wholesale markets and see how much their herbs cost and set your prices accordingly. Perhaps you could offer the herbs at a slightly cheaper rate or at a discount if you have an ongoing relationship with the restaurant.

Group selling

If your herb-selling takes off, you may want to get friends involved by forming a local herb collective. Each member of the group could be responsible for growing a certain herb to ensure meeting the demand from local buyers.

3 Growing vegetables

With the growing popularity of the 'green theme', people are actively seeking home-grown vegetables and fruits that have not had pesticides or herbicides used on them. If you have a huge garden with some space, or can rent some suitable land, consider this money-making idea. And remember it is one the whole family can participate in.

What to offer

You will be growing vegetables and/or fruit to sell directly to customers or to supply your local delicatessen or greengrocer with produce they can promote as 'home-grown'. There are three ways to sell the vegetables directly.

- Go to a weekend market and set up your own stall.
- Advertise in the local paper telling people about your produce. One idea is to have a home-grown fruit and vegetable garage sale on Saturdays and Sundays. You will be amazed by the number of people who will come to have a look.
- You can also try the local restaurants. Because your produce is home-grown, many will be interested.

What you need

- a large garden, allotment or small-holding for growing the produce
- a selection of seeds that are in season
- a good water supply
- the knowledge and determination to weed and care for the plants organically or with a minimum of pesticides
- spade, fork, hoe and rake
- a phone and a mobile phone or pager
- business cards, fliers and leaflets detailing your range of produce
- a diary
- a receipt book
- a T-shirt or sweatshirt advertising your business

Getting started

If you are going to sell directly, advertise in the local paper or, alternatively, book a stall at the local market. Remember to have a float of about £50 in change if you are selling directly. If you are going to put up a sign on the roadside near your home, make sure it's neat and in large colourful letters. Emphasise the words 'fresh' and 'home-grown'.

In the UK, unless you have been formally given an 'organic' sticker by government authorities or the Soil Association, you can't easily promote your produce as 'organic'. You can, however, push the home-grown element of your produce.

What to charge

It is important to do your research – find out what vegetables and fruit are in demand, their prices and where you fit in the market. What you charge will depend largely on prices at your local wholesale market. As a guide, take the wholesale figure and add on 10–20 per cent, because your product is home-grown, fresh and local.

4 Window boxes

In the inner cities, where people tend to live in units and flats, window boxes are undergoing a revival. However, most people don't have the time to go out and buy the window box, plant the seeds and then wait for them to grow and bloom. They would rather buy the box with flowers and plants already growing. This may be the perfect chance for you to corner the window-box market.

What to offer

You will be selling window boxes complete with plants at markets.

What you need

- window boxes bought in quantity directly from the manufacturer
- paints, paint brushes and varnish to decorate the window boxes
- soil and fertiliser mix
- a supply of seeds or seedlings (both flowering plants and herbs)
- a portfolio of photos of window boxes you have sold
- a phone and a mobile phone or pager
- business cards, fliers and leaflets detailing your rates and services, with a list of prices and sizes of boxes you offer
- a diary
- a receipt book and an order book

Getting started

First, buy a selection of window boxes wholesale from the manufacturer. Then decorate them by painting them in popular home colours.

You could start out doing theme boxes, for example a sweet-smelling herb box, a spicy-smelling herb box, a flower box and a miniature vegetable box. The herb and miniature vegetable boxes will be popular with cooks and look great on kitchen window sills.

Once the seedlings are growing, take the sample boxes to the market and see how they sell. Be prepared to take orders. People may want a certain mix of plants, herbs or vegetables. You could also take the boxes to your local nursery and see if they are interested in stocking them. Try visiting church groups, women's groups, senior citizens' associations and sporting clubs to ask if you can speak at their next meeting and show them your wares.

What to charge

Your price will depend on the cost of the window box itself and the plants and seedlings. Your prices should start at around £15 per box, taking into account the amount of effort you have to put into making each box. Charge more if the plants are exotic or fully developed.

5 Weeding

People love to make their gardens grow, but sometimes the battle with the weeds gets to be too much. Now, you are probably thinking that if you looked in the gardening section of the classifieds, you would see many advertisements for weeding and gardening services. But remember that those advertisers service their own areas, they may not be available when the client wants them (availability is crucial these days) and it may just be that your advertisement stands out more than others.

What to offer

You will offer to weed clients' gardens regularly.

What you need

- overalls or garden work gear

- a garden spade, a garden fork, a rake and a hoe
- work gloves
- environmentally friendly weedkiller
- a phone and a mobile phone or pager (or an answering machine)
- business cards, fliers and leaflets detailing your rates and services
- a diary, to keep track of appointments
- a receipt book
- a T-shirt advertising your business

Getting started

Put an advertisement in the local paper in the gardening section, and posters up at shopping centres. Ask your local nursery if you can put up a sign there. Also visit local senior citizens groups: they may be interested in hearing about your service.

What to charge

Start by charging about £10 an hour. If you are working for a pensioner, offer a discount. Don't forget to have some fliers or business cards made and ask your clients to pass them on to their friends.

6 Mobile mulcher

Garden clippings, lopped tree branches and weeds can make quite a mess. I used to throw the lot onto the compost heap, or if they were just too big, it was time for a trip to the tip. A mobile mulching service will prove popular in any neighbourhood.

What to offer

You will offer a mobile mulching service. You will either hire or buy a portable mulching machine, and go around to people's homes to mulch up their waste and spread it on their garden. This is definitely good for the environment. Just make sure you don't mulch up a noxious weed which is then going to thrive in every corner of the garden. You will need to have some knowledge of botany or be guided by the householder.

What you need

- a portable mulcher, hired or purchased
- a selection of garden tools and saws
- overalls
- gloves
- protective glasses
- a van, or a car and trailer for the mulching machine and tools
- a magnetic sign for the side of your car or van
- a phone and a mobile phone or pager
- business cards, fliers and leaflets detailing your rates and services
- a diary
- a receipt book
- a T-shirt advertising your business

Getting started

The best way to attract clients is via an advertisement in the local paper. Think of a cute name for your service – something like 'Mrs Mobile Mulch' will attract attention. Emphasise personal service and the 'greenness' of your business. Advertisements at garden centres and hardware stores will also attract attention.

Contact gardening groups in your suburb and let them know about your service. Schools, hospitals and other organisations with large gardens may be interested in hearing from you. Church groups, women's groups and sporting clubs also present an opportunity to spread the word. Do a letter-box drop around your neighbourhood and advertise in the local newspaper.

You must sort out whether you hire your mulcher or buy one. Hiring for a few months is a good idea because if the business doesn't work out (highly unlikely with this enterprise) you can return the mulcher.

A mulcher can vary in price depending on whether it is large or small, new or second hand. Do a ring around of stores and get a competitive price on purchase and hire.

Make sure your trailer is colourful and your business name and phone number are displayed so all can see.

If you have a clever name for your business, you should send out a press release to local papers – it may catch the eye of the gardening writer or the general reporter looking for an upbeat human interest story or positive 'benefit-busting' yarn.

What to charge

Take into account your costs: the mulcher, fliers, sign writing on the trailer and phone expenses. So, about £15 an hour is a good price. Most jobs will take about an hour.

——— 7 Growing exotic flowers ———

Exotic flowers are immensely popular as gifts. They tend to be expensive, and can be difficult to get hold of, so this is a great opportunity for dedicated green-fingered enthusiasts to diversify.

What to offer

If you have the suitable facilities you will be growing exotic flowers and plants as an extra component of your usual horticulturist activities, and will sell them to local florists and at the markets. Even if you only have a heated greenhouse you can grow a large range of exotic plants, some of which are hardier than you might think.

What you need

- suitable facilities and space to grow the plants
- shovels, hoes, cultivation equipment and a water supply
- a legal supply of exotic seeds or seedlings
- a licence from the appropriate authority if the plants you grow are protected in some way
- packaging material
- a means of transporting your flowers to market
- a phone and a mobile phone or pager
- business cards, fliers and leaflets showing photos of your flowers and their prices
- a diary
- a receipt book
- a T-shirt advertising your business

Getting started

First, find out which exotic flowers are in demand in your area but are in short supply. Then find the plants on that list which can grow in your climate. You can do this by talking to florists and nurseries or the organisations representing these groups. You should also contact the Ministry of Agriculture, Fisheries and Food to find out if they have any special rules and regulations that affect you.

You will need to research packaging for the flowers, to prevent any damage during shipment. When your flowers are ready to be sold on, you can take them to wholesale flower markets or offer them to individual florists and nurseries.

Remember this is a business that requires a great deal of time and nurturing on your part. Exotic or unusual plants can be hard to grow and pests can be a problem. It is best to try this business out as a sideline to your other work before plunging large amounts of capital into it. It will also depend on what flowers and plants your local florist needs.

What to charge

Your price will depend on the wholesale price of flowers where you live and the costs you have incurred in producing your batch of exotics. A visit to the wholesale markets should give you a good idea of prices. Remember, the more flowers you sell in a high-volume deal, the more affordable your product becomes.

——— 8 Sprouting-head maker ———

Have you ever been to the markets and seen sprouted heads made out of old tights or stockings? They have faces made from buttons and their hair is real grass growing through the fabric. They are favourites with the young and the old and are cheap to make.

What to offer

You will be making the sprouted or grassy heads and selling them at markets.

What you need

- a supply of used tights or stockings
- fertile soil and sawdust
- grass seeds
- buttons or toy eyes
- jewellery, to decorate female sprouted heads
- table, chair and umbrella for market stall
- leaflets telling people how to care for grassy heads
- photos of grassy heads with various lengths of hair
- a phone and a mobile phone or pager
- business cards, fliers and leaflets detailing your rates and services
- a diary
- a receipt book
- a T-shirt advertising your business

Getting started

First, make a selection of sprouted heads. To make them, sprinkle a handful of grass seeds into the foot of a stocking, then fill the stocking with some sawdust and soil or compost. Mould the sprouted head into a round shape, then tie off the bottom with string or simply knot the stocking.

Next, shape the face. Using a needle and thread, sew on the button eyes, and stitch to form the stocking ears and nose. Add jewellery to the girl sprouted heads. You can try eye patches for the boys.

The sprouted heads should be sold with instructions. People should keep the heads moist and in the sun. Owners should trim the grass regularly so it continues to grow.

You can also name your grassy or sprouted heads and include a 'birth or growth certificate' with each purchase.

Then take the grassy heads to market. A poster with photos would be helpful to show people what the grassy heads look like when grown. Have a fully grown grassy head on your stand so people realise how cute they are.

What to charge

A basic grassy head should sell for about £5. A grassy head decorated with earrings or other fancy gear can be sold for up to £10. You can also sell grassy head families and grassy heads which have little dresses and shirts. Your imagination is your only limit.

9 Maintaining graves

If you go for a walk through your local cemetery you will probably find hundreds of overgrown graves. Sadly, many families lack the time to keep relatives' graves in order. Also, many families have moved away and find it difficult to make regular visits to keep graves tidy. However, the notion of a relative's grave being neglected and unkempt is disturbing to many people.

As setting up a small business is all about tapping into an under-exploited market, give some thought to grave maintenance. Quite a few people these days are earning extra spending money this way.

What to offer

Your job is to keep graves clean, tidy, well presented and cared for. You will be responsible for keeping moss and grime off the head-stones, polishing nameplates and ensuring that the grave has fresh flowers.

What you need

- a uniform – a T-shirt and jeans or shorts are probably best
- a bucket, spade and rake
- cleaning brushes and sponges
- rubber gloves
- metal polish and some soft rags
- flowers from a wholesaler – or grow some yourself to save on costs
- a phone and a mobile phone or pager
- business cards, fliers and leaflets detailing your rates and services
- a diary
- a receipt book

Getting started

First check with your local church and local authority or council to see if there are any regulations governing grave maintenance or access to the cemetery for a money-making scheme. Then start by advertising in the local paper. Think of a catchy name, but don't be too clever – this is a serious job, and you are dealing with people's emotions.

Put up a poster at the local cemetery, as well as on community notice boards. You may be able to pick up some business from local genealogists – people researching family trees frequently discover ancestors buried in distant towns. In these cases, they rely on cleaners to maintain the graves.

Contact local church groups to see if they have any advice on how to get your message to people.

Remember, this small business is an unusual one, so the local media may be interested in doing a story on it. Contact radio, newspaper and television newsrooms and talk to the local news editor or editor-in-chief. Follow up with a one-page brief on your service.

What to charge

A completely overgrown grave will take you about two hours to clean on your first visit. After that, you'll probably spend about half an hour per visit. Use the following as a guide.

- overgrown-grave visit – two hours at £10 a visit, plus £5 for flowers
- follow-up visits – £5–10
- reasonably tidy graves, maintenance visit – £5

Don't forget senior citizen discounts, as well as quantity discounts in cases involving a number of family plots.

One lady who set up this business chose to wear a bright pink uniform. She said it was a happy job looking after people's dear departed.

13

CLEANING AND CLEARING

---

1 Washing clothes

Let's face it, many of us resent the time spent on doing the washing so if you have a talent in the laundry and some spare time here is a job for you.

What to offer

You will be taking in people's washing by the bag or basketful. Clients can drop off bags at your house in the morning and pick up the washed and folded clothes that evening. Or, you can pick up and deliver for a bit extra.

What you need

- a sturdy washing machine
- a clothesline or drier
- washing powder (make sure it is environmentally friendly)
- starch
- fabric softener
- stain remover
- a phone and a mobile phone or pager
- business cards, fliers and leaflets detailing your rates and services
- a diary

- an order book
- a receipt book
- a T-shirt or sweatshirt advertising your business – publicity is important

Getting started

You can advertise in the local paper and put posters up at the shopping centre. Contact professional women's groups and tell them about your service. Try asking local church halls, community centres and child-minding centres to hand out leaflets. Consider a letter-box drop around your neighbourhood and the business area.

Make sure the leaflets tell people exactly what you're offering, and list your range of charges. Try contacting people who advertise ironing services in your local paper. You may be able to develop a mutually beneficial arrangement: you tell people about their ironing service and they tell people about your washing service.

Make sure that you don't mix up different clients' clothes, that the socks don't disappear in the washing machine Bermuda Triangle and that the whites don't end up pink.

What to charge

Charge by the basketful. Set your basket prices from £5 or charge by weight, so one kilogram (2 lb) of washing may cost £3 to wash.

Remember to offer senior citizen discounts or 'family rates' for three or more baskets. If you are picking up and delivering in your area, add a bit extra to the final bill to cover your costs.

2 Ironing

Many people just don't have the time to iron. In large families, it isn't the most important priority and a huge pile of ironing usually builds up in the corner of the family room – a testament to the lack of spare time.

Now you are probably saying there are already a lot of people offering to do ironing. Well, yes there are, but that doesn't mean you can't carve out your own niche market. I know one couple who set up their own ironing service, offering home pick-up and delivery, and they have been inundated with work.

What to offer

You will be doing ironing by the bag or basketful. People will drop off their wrinkled clothes in the morning and you will have them ironed by the time they finish work that evening. If you really want to attract customers, offer a pick-up and delivery service for your area.

What you need

- a reliable iron (or rotary iron or steam presser) that doesn't mark
- an ironing board
- spray starch or water
- a supply of wire coat hangers
- needle and thread (in case a button falls off)
- stain remover
- transport
- a phone and a mobile phone or pager, and an answering machine
- business cards, fliers and leaflets detailing your rates and services
- a diary
- a receipt book
- a T-shirt advertising your business

Getting started

The best way to build up your clientele is to advertise in the local suburban paper. Think of a catchy name or phrase, for example 'Ironing Inc', 'The Awesome Ironing Machine' or 'The Wrinkle Eradicator'. Perhaps you could have the newspaper put an iron symbol on your advertisement. Posters at the shopping centre will also help.

Contact professional women's groups and let them know about your service – many women who work full-time are still trying to run the household by themselves. Try contacting local child-care groups and ask them if they would hand out leaflets to working parents who might want to use your service.

Ask the local laundromat if you can put up a poster or if they might consider you as a contract ironer. If you are offering a mobile service, you could get a magnetic sign made for your car door – more advertising can't hurt.

What to charge

Most people charge by the bag or basketful. Your rates should be no lower than about £6–12 a basket. Add an extra £3 for pick-up and delivery. You can also charge by weight – about £3 per kilogram (£1.50–2 per pound weight).

3 Window cleaning

Modern homes have lots of windows, flooding rooms with sunlight. But lots of windows mean lots of cleaning. Many home owners put window cleaning in the 'too hard' category or simply stand outside the house and give the exterior a blast with the garden hose. There is definitely a market for competent window cleaning.

What to offer

You will be offering to wash people's windows, including stained glass windows, sliding doors and, if need be, skylights. You can offer to clean all bathroom and hallway mirrors as well.

What you need

- a ladder
- a bucket, a squeegee, rags and washcloths
- newspaper – great for cleaning mirrors
- window cleaner – try using an environmentally friendly cleaner with a lemon or tea-tree base, which can be bought wholesale from your local health or 'green' shop

- a spray container
- a scrubbing brush
- a toothbrush or nail brush to clean grime from stained glass windows
- a file of references plus 'before and after' pictures of windows to show clients
- transport
- phone, mobile phone, pager or answering machine
- business cards, fliers and leaflets detailing your rates and services
- a diary
- a receipt book
- a T-shirt advertising your business

Getting started

The first stop is your local paper to put in an advertisement. Give your business a warm, friendly name that will attract clients, or personalise the service – 'Mark's Window Cleaning'. Put up signs at the local supermarket and at hardware stores or other outlets selling supplies for home renovation. Try a letter-box drop around your neighbourhood. Ask any friendly shop owners in the vicinity if you can leave a batch of fliers. You could offer them a one-off free window cleaning in return. They might even become regular customers.

Consider contacting estate agents in your suburb: many look after rental properties and will add you to their 'resource list' of various cleaners and tradespeople. Also contact the Tenants' Association, Management Committee or equivalent at large blocks of flats in your neighbourhood to see if they are interested. Senior citizen groups and professional organisations may also be interested in hearing from you. You could try making contact with builders and building firms who may need you to come in and clean windows after they have finished construction of homes.

What to charge

First find out what your potential competition is charging then set your rates accordingly.

You can either charge by the hour on small jobs like flats and town houses, or quote an all-inclusive figure. Hourly rates should be

£10–20. Charge an all-inclusive rate for a three-bedroom house, from £6. You could try a three-month reduced rate to clean the windows once a month. Don't forget to offer pensioner discounts.

Offer free quotations. This will give you a chance to check the windows and to show references to the prospective clients.

—— 4 Mobile car valeting ——

For many people, washing and cleaning out the car is an irksome task that they never seem to have time for. If you are good at this job why not set up a mobile car-cleaning service?

What to offer

You will visit people's homes or workplaces and valet their cars for them. You can offer a range of services, from a basic wash to a full valet.

What you need

- transport
- car cleaning products
- a phone and a mobile phone or pager
- business cards, fliers and leaflets detailing your rates and services
- a diary
- a receipt book
- a T-shirt advertising your business

Getting started

First, advertise in the car section of the local paper. Many people often want their car valeted before they sell it. Visit major parking areas and put fliers under car windscreens. Put posters up in buildings where lots of people work. Anywhere that people park their cars is a great place for you to advertise. You must emphasise you come to the client in their office and you clean their car while they work. This service is definitely a money-maker.

Ask your clients to tell their friends or put your fliers on their office notice boards.

What to charge

This will depend on what drive-in car washes are offering at garages and service centres. Here are some suggestions.

- basic wash and clean – £10
- basic wash and polish – £15
- full valet – £40

——— 5 Lorry and bus washing ———

There are a lot of large lorries and buses on our roads – and their owners pride themselves on keeping them clean and shiny. But when they're tired after a long haul, cleaning the lorry is probably the last thing on their minds.

Many large towns and cities have long-distance lorry driver cafés on their outskirts. You may find a mobile lorry or bus cleaning business could prove to be a winner.

What to offer

You will be offering to clean and polish lorries and buses.

What you need

- car- and truck-cleaning equipment: brushes, cloths, washing liquid, car polish and tyre blacking
- mops and brushes on long poles, for those hard-to-get-at spots
- hoses
- buckets
- transport
- a phone or pager
- business cards, fliers and leaflets detailing your rates and services
- posters to put up at truck stops

- a diary
- a receipt book
- overalls and T-shirts advertising your business

Getting started

First, spread the word that you are available at certain times of the week to wash and clean lorries and buses and that you can also be booked for special cleaning sessions. Then visit garages that sell fuel to lorry and bus drivers and contact big companies that use buses and lorries and tell them about your service.

You can also put advertisements up at cafés on main highways and motorways where lorry drivers stop, and offer to clean their vehicles while they eat.

Important fact

This is a job which should not be done alone. For your personal safety make sure you and a friend are involved and never wash lorries at night.

What to charge

You should have a set of rates based on the type of washing or cleaning you are required to do. Here are some suggestions.

- outside wash – £20
- outside wash and polish – £30
- outside and inside cleaning – £30
- deluxe cleaning – £50

6 Garage busters

There are many people who have messy garages and are always planning to clean them up, but never get the time. So if you like cleaning why not become your neighbourhood garage buster?

What to offer

You will offer to come in and clean out garages. You will throw out rubbish. You will sweep and clean the garage and, if need be, paint the inside.

What you need

- a van, or a car and trailer
- a magnetic sign for your car and trailer – the more advertising, the better
- overalls and gloves
- mops, brooms, buckets, detergent and cardboard boxes for repacking
- a phone and a mobile phone or pager
- business cards, fliers and leaflets detailing your rates and services
- a diary
- a receipt book

Getting started

The first thing to do is to advertise in the local paper and put posters up at local shopping centres. Posters at child-care centres and advertisements in school papers will help. You should send out press releases because this sort of wacky idea may attract some media interest. Letter-box drops may also help attract customers.

Discuss with your client what is rubbish and what isn't. Recycle as much as possible.

This is the sort of job that is ideal for two people – garages can be full of rubbish and heavy lifting may be involved.

What to charge

For this sort of service, charge £10–15 an hour, depending on how big the job is and if you have someone helping. You may have to charge extra for disposing of weedkiller, old car batteries and other hazardous materials at toxic waste deposits.

——— 7 Roof gutter cleaning ———

This is definitely a money-maker for people who are not afraid of heights! Roof gutters often become blocked, and cleaning them can be a time-consuming job. If you don't mind getting dirty, you should consider giving this one a go.

What to offer

You will be offering to clean people's gutters. This will include scrubbing them clean and disinfecting them to get rid of smells. You will also offer to cut back the branches of overhanging trees which cause half the problem, as their leaves fall directly into the gutter.

What you need

- a ladder
- a hose, just in case the house hasn't got one
- plastic sheeting (to spread on the ground so you can fling the muck from the gutter onto it and easily clean up afterwards)
- a tree saw and a small chain saw (for lopping branches of overhanging trees)
- a bucket
- scrubbing brushes
- disinfectant – use one with a lemon or tea-tree base
- overalls
- gloves
- a face mask – sometimes, the smell can be unpleasant
- insurance – check with your insurer or local authority to see if you need cover
- transport
- a phone and a mobile phone, pager or answering machine
- business cards, fliers and leaflets detailing your rates and services
- a diary
- a receipt book
- a T-shirt advertising your business

Getting started

First, check with your local council to see if there are any regulations regarding heavy pruning or lopping of trees, hedges and bushes.

Place an advertisement in your local paper and ask local hardware and home renovation stores if you can put up a poster and leave some fliers. Knock on doors or do a letter-box drop in your neighbourhood, particularly at the peak times of autumn and spring. Leave fliers at the local day nursery, nursery school or playgroup. Contact senior citizen groups and tell them about your service. Make contact with builders in the area and tell them about your service – they may tell their clients.

Remember, people like to be able to contact you straight away. If you already have an answering machine, consider buying or hiring a mobile phone as well, so that you are always only a phone call away.

What to charge

Set your rates at £10 an hour, and don't forget to offer discounts to senior citizens. If you have to lop tree branches, charge a few pounds extra for the use of the chain saw.

14
TOURISTS SERVICES

1 Immigrant welcomer and interpreter

When someone arrives in a new country either as an immigrant or for an extended working holiday, it can be tough finding accommodation, settling in and understanding the culture. So if you are a great organiser and perhaps speak a second language, this service is worth a try. When I moved to London for a twelve-month stay the first few weeks were terrible, finding housing, getting phones and power connected and just fitting in. I should have loved some help and would gladly have paid for it.

What to offer

You will be offering to help newcomers from the moment they get off the plane. This may include meeting them, helping them decide where they want to live, sorting out utilities, helping them buy a car, finding schools for the children and introducing them to new friends.

If they are from a non-English-speaking background you may also be required to act as an interpreter and to suggest language programmes and other ways to improve their English.

This sort of business suits someone from the same cultural background as those they are welcoming.

What you need

- respect within your community
- the ability to speak a second language
- an understanding of the stresses and problems people face when they first arrive in a new country
- booklets you can hand out to newcomers, written in their own language, about what to expect in their new country
- a list of services and contacts useful to newcomers
- contacts with social groups that newcomers may want to join
- transport
- insurance, if you are transporting clients in your own car
- a phone and a mobile phone or pager
- business cards, fliers and leaflets detailing your rates and services
- a diary
- a receipt book

Getting started

First, talk to community leaders and groups about the service you want to offer. It is best to target people from one or two specific countries. For example if you speak Cantonese, contact Chinese community leaders and target people moving from Hong Kong to your country. You'll need their support because they can help you spread the word and recommend you to newcomers.

Also contact council and government agencies dealing with immigration and tell them about your service. See if you can put up posters there, as well as at community centres. Then put advertisements in local newspapers for ethnic minority groups (for example, the local Italian paper or Chinese paper). People who read these papers may want to use your services or may know of others who would be interested. Try to advertise in overseas papers. Target native language papers and be precise about the service you offer.

Contact local travel agents and tell them about your service. They may have clients or overseas contacts who can help spread the word.

Don't forget the back-packer market. There are many Australians and New Zealanders who head to London, for example, for a twelve-month working holiday. These people may need your help. You could advertise in travel magazines in Australia and New Zealand and contact back-packing organisations to help spread the word. You could get in contact with visiting Australians and New Zealanders in London, who may spread the word as well.

What to charge

Your fees will depend largely on the length of time you spend with the family or persons who have just arrived. Try setting half-daily, daily and weekly rates. Take into account the cost of your car, phone and other expenses. Start around £50 for a half-day, and go up to £100 for a full day helping a family. Weekly rates should start around £300–400 plus expenses.

——— 2 Guided walking tours ———

For holiday-makers and tourists, guided tours are the perfect way to get a close-up look at their holiday destination. If you like walking and have a flare for history then consider this as a money-making option.

What to offer

You will be offering tourists personalised guided tours or group walks through the local area, which are not offered by the local tourist organisation or tour companies. Remember to emphasise that you're offering people a chance to view the area from the locals' point of view. You should show them places they wouldn't normally see.

On weekends and during peak holiday times, have regular group tours that leave at the same time from the same spot. That way, people visiting the area will be able to join up with a regular advertised tour at set times and places.

Most of your guided walks should last for one hour, in consideration of those who might be elderly or unfit. Personalised tours can go for longer periods, depending on the group and their specific requests.

You should also consider what type of specialised tour you will offer. For example in London you could offer a walking tour of the favourite haunts of Diana, Princess of Wales, or in other areas a tour of unusual historical sites. Try to find something that interests you and develop a walking tour around that concept.

What you need

- a thorough knowledge of your area
- an ability to get along with people
- sturdy walking shoes
- a hat and sunscreen
- a series of planned walks, each slightly different from the others
- a knapsack
- a first-aid kit (just in case)
- a phone and a mobile phone or pager or an answering machine
- business cards, fliers and leaflets detailing your rates and services
- a diary
- a receipt book
- a T-shirt or sweatshirt advertising your business

Getting started

First contact your local tourist association and find out if there are any rules governing the running of tours in your area. You might, for example, have to join the tourist association to get a local tour guide accreditation. Then advertise in tourist publications. Contact the local tourist centre and let the staff know about your service; ask them to put up posters and hand out fliers. Contact all major hotels in your area and tell them about your service. Ask them if you can put a flier in the information kit available in each room.

Find out where most of your tourists come from. If it is a large city, consider advertising in major newspapers in that area, so that people planning to visit your area can book ahead.

If you can, put up posters at railway stations, bus depots and airports. Many of them have notice boards for posters and fliers. Some also have special areas set aside for brochures.

Contact local special-interest groups in your town, and the Youth Hostel Association.

What to charge

For group walks lasting an hour, charge about £5 per person. For personalised walks, you can charge more, especially if the walk is being tailored to the client's needs. For one or two people, charge £8–10 each. For larger groups charge a group rate. Put a price on your knowledge of your area – don't undersell your skill as a guide and communicator.

3 Antique tours

In the UK and Europe there is a lot of interest in buying and collecting antiques. Tourists and locals all want the best buy possible. So if you share this interest why not consider running antique auction tours but with a slight twist!

What to offer

You will be running regular antique tours to antique fairs, auctions and businesses.

What you need

- a knowledge of forthcoming antique and clearance auctions in your area
- a knowledge of antiques and antique prices (not compulsory but an advantage)
- transport (a car or a minibus)
- insurance
- a phone and a mobile phone or pager
- business cards, fliers and leaflets detailing your rates and services
- professionally made posters advertising your tours
- a diary
- a receipt book
- a T-shirt advertising your business

Getting started

First, find out where and when the big sales and auctions are being held. The big auction houses will most likely have monthly auction days. Contact estate agents handling farm properties: they will know which auctioneers are handling forthcoming clearances. Don't forget police auctions of seized and lost property – you never know what you might find. The same goes for sales of goods seized by Customs.

Consider brushing up your knowledge of antiques. People will ask you questions and you should be able to provide intelligent answers. Local colleges are likely to run such courses.

Think about how you are going to transport your clients around. Start small and use your own car for the first couple of runs. This will limit you to four clients, but it's a chance to get a feel for how the business will go. Check with your insurance company to find out if using your car for this sort of purpose increases the insurance costs.

Then, put an advertisement in the paper, and posters at local shopping centres. Contact your local tourist information centre and let the staff know you offer this service – people visiting your town or city may be interested in taking your tour.

Consider asking major hotels in your town if you can put fliers in guest rooms as a way of promoting your service. It's the dream of many tourists visiting the UK and Europe to come away with an antique treasure – your service will give them a chance to break away from the often expensive antique stores and do some real treasure hunting of their own.

You should also consider organising tours to specific types of antique auctions. For example on one tour you might visit only jewellery auctions, another might be furniture, a third might be for antique clothes.

Clearance auctions in your area

These are not only auctions run by the big antique sellers but auctions where antique dealers themselves go to buy. These auctions are usually advertised in national, regional and local papers. They might be farm clearance sales, deceased estates and so on.

If you keep the numbers down to four people per tour you can use your own car. If you want to be more adventurous, look into hiring a small van or bus or, better still, do a deal with a local bus-rental company.

What to charge

Your price will depend on how far you have to travel and how many auctions you go to. A day tour should start at around £30–60 per person. This fee should include lunch: you could do a deal with one of the pubs or cafés along the way.

—— 4 Bargain-shopping guide ——

For tourists and other visitors in a strange town or city who may not know where to find the cheapies, bargain-hunting can be a problem. The answer – hire a bargain-shopping guide.

What to offer

You will offer to work as a bargain-shopping guide. You will take groups of two or three people on shopping tours. This will mean taking them to various discount shops, seconds stores, factory outlets and so forth.

What you need

- a knowledge of bargain stores in your area, including shops that sell clothes, linen, china, glassware and shoes
- an ability to get along with people
- a pair of comfortable shoes
- a car, or you can use public transport
- insurance, if you have a car and will be driving clients around
- a phone and a mobile phone or pager
- business cards, fliers and leaflets detailing your rates and services
- a diary
- a receipt book
- a T-shirt advertising your business

Getting started

First, track down all the bargain shops in your area and visit each one. Ask the owners if they will offer your shoppers a discount if you regularly bring people to the store.

You should also check with your car insurance company. You may need extra cover if you will be taking people around in your car. If you are using your own car, get a magnetic door sign for extra advertising.

Advertise in tourist magazines and contact local hotels and bed-and-breakfast operators. Tell them about your service and ask if you can put leaflets in the foyer or, better still, leaflets in each room.

Contact travel agencies and tell them about your service. Ask if they will recommend their clients to you.

Don't forget that local people may also want to use your service. You should advertise in local papers, put up signs at shopping centres and let sporting and social groups know about what you can offer.

What to charge

Charge per half-day or full day, aiming at about £20 for a full day.

15

A WAY WITH ANIMALS?

1 Puppy training

Little puppies can be big nightmares. Although they are cute, they can also ruin furniture, cause chaos on the carpet and be disobedient. And, as any dog-lover knows, early obedience training is important if you are to enjoy your pet's company.

What to offer

Offer to run regular puppy-training courses over four-week periods. For two hours weekly you will instruct your group of puppies and their new owners in basic commands, puppy health and puppy first aid.

What you need

- experience in training puppies (Taking an adult education course on animal welfare or animal care is a good idea before starting this sort of enterprise.)
- a regular meeting place for weekly classes
- certificates for puppies completing the course
- puppy treats, to facilitate training
- a course book for owners, explaining the training (These books should be designed so that owners can take notes and keep a record of their pet's progress.)

- a portfolio, with references from previous clients
- transport
- a phone and a mobile phone or pager
- business cards, fliers and leaflets detailing your rates and services
- a diary
- a receipt book
- a T-shirt advertising your business

Getting started

First you'll probably want to enrol in a course in animal training and care. The next step is to devise a basic puppy-training course. The course should include teaching the puppies such basic commands as 'sit', 'lie', 'heel' and so forth. The puppies should be taught to walk on a leash, and owners should be taught the basics in puppy health and first aid.

You may want to have a vet or a veterinary nurse be a guest speaker on these subjects. Also, devise a basic puppy course book which includes a diary that owners can fill out during the course.

Before you launch your business, try your course out on a few friends who have pets. You'll gain experience and will get an idea of the kind of problems that might arise.

When you're ready to launch, advertise your course in the local paper. Tell pet shops and local dog breeders and dog-breeding associations about your course. Ask them to help hand out leaflets and business cards. Also visit local vets and tell them about your service. You can invite them to be guest speakers. Also ask if you can put up posters in their surgery.

Write to pet food companies and tell them about your course – you never know, they may send you sample products to hand out at your classes.

What to charge

The cost of the course will depend on class numbers, your experience and any guest speakers you have in. Keep class numbers to between five and eight pairs of pets and owners. Classes should run for two hours once a week over a three-to-four week period.

Try starting rates of £30–50 for a four-week course including certificate and doggie diary.

---

2 Dog-walking

Quality time spent walking the dog is fast becoming a thing of the past. We work long hours, leaving the unfortunate pet moping on the back step alone and unexercised. Have I created a miserable enough picture for you? If so, it is time you tried earning cash as a Super Walker – walking pet dogs whose owners have deserted them for the office.

What to offer

You'll be offering a regular walking service for dogs. You will go to the client's house and take the dog for a good long walk and play in the park. Some dogs may require walking each day, others may just have to be taken on a good long run twice a week.

What you need

- an affinity with dogs
- a collection of doggie toys (frisbee, ball, stick)
- doggie treats (from the pet shop)
- references and if possible a police check
- a van, if feasible, so that you can collect a group of pooches and walk them all at once (assuming they get along with each other)
- a phone and a mobile phone or pager
- business cards, fliers and leaflets detailing your rates and services
- a diary
- a receipt book
- a T-shirt advertising your business

Getting started

An advertisement in the local paper is a good place to start. Posters at supermarkets and at pet shops will also help. Try contacting your local vet and telling the staff about your service – perhaps they will let you put up a poster. Also contact senior citizens' groups: members who are not very mobile may find it difficult to walk their dogs. Try putting up posters in office blocks in your area.

What to charge

Your rates will depend on how regularly you walk the dogs. Most walks take at least an hour. If you get a group of dogs together you will make more per hour. You should consider weekly rates with discounts for pensioners. Here are some suggested rates.

- walking the dog five days a week – £30
- walking the dog two days a week – £15
- walking the dog once a week – £10

Important fact

This job brings with it responsibility. Caring for someone's pet is not to be taken lightly. References are essential and you always need to keep a close eye on your animal charges.

If you intend to service more than one dog per day, you should mention to the owner the need for regular and up-to-date vaccinations against communicable diseases, and ask to see a current vaccination certificate.

———— 3 Pet-diet controller ————

There are many well-loved and over indulged pets in this world. In fact new research has revealed that 25–35 per cent of British pets alone are overweight. So if you have some animal health-care training then a pet-diet controller may just be the business for you to set up.

What to offer

You will be helping dogs and cats lose weight. You will also be educating the owner on how best to care for their pet and what diets will stop them getting so chubby. This includes helping to exercise the pet regularly, helping to shop for the right food and teaching the owner to say 'No!' to over indulgence.

What you need

- animal health care skills or training
- information leaflets on why pets get fat and how best to tackle the problem
- a portfolio containing before and after shots of pets which have lost weight
- references
- transport
- a phone and a mobile phone or pager
- business cards, fliers and leaflets detailing your rates and services
- a diary
- a receipt book
- a T-shirt advertising your business

Getting started

Enrol in an animal-care course if you don't have the skills or if you need to update your expertise.

Contact local pet clubs, dog and cat breeders and tell them about your service. Also posters at pet stores, shopping centres and town notice boards may attract attention, as will an advertisement in the local paper and newsletters put together by cat and dog breeders.

Tell the local vet about your service and, if he agrees to help you, ask if you can leave some fliers.

What to charge

You can charge in a range of ways. A one-off consultation to put together a diet plan and exercise plan should cost the client £25–40. If you are to make regular visits to walk the pet and ensure it is sticking to the diet then offer the client five visits for around £100.

Important fact

This is a business which requires expertise and training on your part. Make sure you get that training as the health of an animal is involved.

4 Pet beautician

Pet care is becoming extremely trendy. In fact, many vets recommend regular pet care as part of a pet's life and overall well-being. For this reason pet beauticians are becoming extremely popular. If you are good with animals, why not consider cashing in as a pet beautician?

What to offer

You will be offering a grooming and washing service for dogs and cats at their homes.

What you need

- a way with animals
- experience clipping and grooming animals (completion of a pet care course would be a big benefit)
- expertise in pet massage (Many older animals, especially those suffering from arthritis, benefit from massage. You should do a course.)
- a collection of brushes, electric clippers, scissors and other supplies for grooming
- pet shampoo
- a collection of towels for drying pets
- a collection of ribbons (for poodles)
- transport
- a phone and a mobile phone or pager
- business cards, fliers and leaflets detailing your rates and services
- a diary
- a receipt book
- a T-shirt advertising your business

Getting started

Enrol in a course in grooming and pet care. You can update your skills and learn the latest techniques. You should also learn pet massage to treat sick or old animals. Once your skills are up to date, put an advertisement in the paper listing your services.

Contact your local paper and radio station; a story about a pet beautician may just interest a jaded journalist. Ask your local shopping centre if you can put up a display one weekend. Bring some animals along and have hourly displays of massage and grooming.

Make sure you have a supply of fliers and business cards to hand out. Contact local vets and tell them about your service. Many vets have pet beauticians working for them one day a week. You may be able to work out a similar arrangement with your local veterinarian. You should also ask if you can leave fliers and put up posters. Contact dog and cat clubs in your area as they may have members who are interested in using your service.

What to charge

Start by setting your rate at around £10 an hour. This will cover grooming, clipping and washing. If the client is a regular one you can offer a three-visit deal. Don't forget a discount for pensioners.

Alternatively, charge per dog. Groom and wash a small dog for £20, a large dog for £30.

5 Pet photography

We all love our pets and our pets love us, but finding someone to take a formal photo of our beloved furry, feathered or scaly friend can be difficult. If you love photography, perhaps you should consider pet portraiture.

What to offer

You will be offering to take formal portraits of pets for their owners. You will also be offering to take formal pictures of stud animals, including cattle and horses.

What you need

- experience in photography
- a reliable 35 mm camera, tripod and flash or portable studio lights

- a selection of coloured backdrops of varying widths and lengths
- experience of working with animals
- a portfolio of various portraits you have taken
- a selection of pet toys
- a selection of pet treats to encourage animals to behave
- transport
- a phone and a mobile phone or pager
- business cards, fliers and leaflets detailing your rates and services
- a diary
- a receipt book
- a T-shirt advertising your business

Getting started

First put together a portfolio of twelve to fifteen pet portraits. Then start drumming up business. Put an advertisement in the pet section of the paper. Put up posters at veterinary clinics, pet shops, animal welfare groups and at the local shopping centre.

Contact local breeding associations (dog, cat, horse, cattle, goat and bird) and tell them about your service. Go to their shows, set up a stand and hand out as many fliers as possible. Set up an outdoor studio at the show and take photos on the spot.

Make sure your service is different. Perhaps you could have some costumes for humans and animals to wear, so you could do 'period' or 'fantasy' portraits. For example, a cowboy outfit for the pet owner and a little cowboy hat for the dog could make your service that little bit different.

What to charge

Most photographers who deal with human subjects charge for the session, then keep the negatives and charge for the prints. You will probably have more success if you charge for the session and then give the negatives to the customer. Offer to have them printed and quote your rates, based on your processing costs. For sessions at animal shows charge special show rates: say £25 a session plus the cost of the film. If you have to go to the house, charge, say, £30 plus the cost of the film. The session should not last any longer than an hour.

Happy snapping!

6 Lost-pet finder

With their notorious curiosity and territorial habits it's not uncommon for pets to go missing. If someone had a central database which was updated daily, tracking down a lost pet would be much easier.

What to offer

You will set up a computer database listing lost pets and those found by the animal welfare agencies and the police. Pet owners will pay you to do a series of searches over a two-week period. You will also offer to put up posters in the area the pet was lost.

What you need

- a love of animals
- contacts with animal welfare groups, police and pet stores
- a computer and computing ability
- access to a photocopier
- a phone and a mobile phone or pager
- business cards, fliers and leaflets detailing your rates and services
- a diary
- a receipt book
- a T-shirt advertising your business

Getting started

First you have to set up your database which allows you to do quick searches according to pet type, breed and area it was lost in. Then contact the animal welfare groups and police and enter the details of the 'found' animals that they have in their care.

Advertise in the pet section in the local paper, put posters and fliers up at pet stores, community centres and in shopping centres. Talk to your local press. Maybe they will consider this a sufficiently unusual idea to deserve some press coverage.

Once someone contacts you, enter their pet details and see if your records have a match. Update your 'found' pet information each day by ringing the animal welfare groups. You can also help clients to put up posters to find their pets and advertise in local papers. You will be surprised by the number of pets that can be located using your database.

One person who set up a business like this found that her success rate was very good. She also discovered that pets can roam a long way from home, so if a dog is lost in Camden Town you need to consider that it may turn up in Chelsea. As the operator of the database you must canvass welfare groups over a wide area.

You then undertake regular searches for your client's pet over a two- to four-week period and charge a set rate per computer search.

What to charge

Here are some suggestions.

- four computer searches over two weeks – £20
- eight computer searches over four weeks – £35
- four computer searches, making 'lost' posters and handing them out to local pet stores etc. – £40

Don't forget to ask clients who are reunited with their pets to write a testimonial and put together a portfolio of happy snaps to show possible clients.

7 Pet taxi

There are many people who have pets but do not have their own transport. They may find it difficult to take their pets to the vet or to visit friends. It might not be possible for them to use a taxi or a bus. So if you have a van and are good with pets consider setting up a pet taxi service.

What to offer

You will offer to transport owners and their pets to appointments.

What you need

- animal handling experience
- a selection of animal carrying cages
- a van or large car
- insurance
- road maps
- a phone and a mobile phone or pager
- business cards, fliers and leaflets detailing your rates and services
- a diary
- a receipt book
- a T-shirt advertising your business

Getting started

First contact your local insurance agency and find out what insurance you need to cover you acting as a taxi service. This is important in case of accidents.

Once you have the van, put an advertisement in the local paper and contact local catteries, kennels and pet breeders around your area. Tell them about your service and leave them leaflets and business cards. Visit local vets and pet shops and ask if you can put up posters and leave business cards. Also, visit senior citizens' organisations and tell them about your service. Their members may be interested in using the pet taxi for visits to the vet.

Consider setting up an information stand at local cat and dog shows to drum up business. Remember, you must get your message out to as many people as possible.

What to charge

The pet taxi service should be on a 'per mile or kilometre' fee basis. Your charge will depend largely on the type of van or car you have and related petrol and maintenance costs. Find out what local taxis and minicabs charge and set your prices accordingly. Your prices can be a little higher because of the particular service you offer. Don't forget to offer discounts to senior citizens.

——————— 8 Holiday pet care ———————

When we go on holiday, our pets often miss out on their usual care and attention. So why not cash in by offering pet owners a holiday for their pet as well? The best part is the pets don't have to leave home. Modern vets are emphasising the importance of making sure that pets are not only well fed, but also happy and contented. This overall care includes their nurturing while their owners are away.

What to offer

You will be offering to walk, feed and care for pets while their owners are away. You will go to the pet owner's home each day to feed the pets, to walk them and to groom or bathe them if necessary. You will be providing owners with the security and comfort of knowing that their much-loved pets are in good hands. You can also offer to ring or write to the clients on holiday, to update them on their pets' care.

You might also offer to water the house plants and bring in the mail and newspaper. The owner would probably be grateful and you can charge a little extra.

What you need

- an affinity with animals is essential
- transport
- an answering machine, pager or, better still, a mobile phone
- references reflecting your trustworthiness, since you'll have access to people's homes
- business cards, fliers and leaflets detailing your rates and services
- a diary
- a receipt book
- a T-shirt or sweatshirt advertising your business

Getting started

Advertise in your local paper under both pet and holiday sections (when people are looking for somewhere to stay, the advertisement will remind them about their pet).

Contact your local veterinary clinics and tell them about your service. If you establish your credibility and legitimacy with them, they may let you put up a poster or may even tell their clients about you.

Consider getting a police check. People feel more comfortable if this is included with your references – after all you will be in their home while they are away.

Visit local pet shops and ask them to let you put up a poster. Local dog clubs, pony clubs and cat and bird fanciers may also be interested in hearing from you. There are many of these clubs around and it doesn't hurt to try them all.

Also consider calling on local travel agencies. It lets them provide yet another service to their customers and helps them anticipate their clients' needs.

What to charge

Your fee depends on the animal you are caring for, how regularly it needs attention and whether you are just feeding it or walking it as well. Here is a guide:

- feed and walk dog (1 week) – £20–£30
- feed only, dog, cat or horse (1 week) – £15–25
- feed bird (three visits per week) – £13

I know a lady who had a high-powered job as a computer programmer, earning a six-figure salary. She gave it up to set up a holiday pet-care business. She is doing very well, earning good money and is considerably less stressed.

9 Pet parties

In this book I suggest a number of money-making schemes linked to pets. This one is perhaps the most unusual.

What to offer

You will organise pet parties so people can get together with their pets and meet other pet owners. You will charge an entry fee and provide the food and atmosphere for the party. People who own similar pets love to get together and swap stories.

What you need

- a park to hold the functions (check with the council to see if pets are allowed)
- fliers and posters advertising your parties
- food and drinks for your parties
- a phone and a mobile phone or pager
- business cards, fliers and leaflets advertising your parties
- a diary
- an order book
- a receipt book

Getting started

First decide on the type of party you will hold. Dog parties are the easiest. Spread the word among local dog owners, go to the area favoured for dog-walking near where you live and hand out fliers, put up posters and spread the word. Ask pet stores if you can put up a poster and even advertise in the pet section in the local paper. Contact dog breeders and let them know. Then set a date – a weekend is the best – and take bookings.

You charge people a fee to attend and for that they get to meet other dog owners, and partake in food and drink. You will need to set up some tables in the local park and take people's fees as they arrive.

You could then try holding bird parties, ferret parties and perhaps mice parties. This business is all about tapping into the need of pet owners to link up with other pet owners

If successful you can also take bookings for special pet birthday parties. I know quite a few people who mark their pet's birthday each year with a small bash – why not tap into that market?

What to charge

You should charge an entry fee of £3–5, depending on what the drinks and food cost. If you get booked to organise special pet parties, charge an overall fee plus the cost of food and drink. An organising fee should be about £20–40.

Happy partying!

10 Pet beds and pet coats

Designer pet products are a big money-spinner in many countries, so making cute pet beds and designer pet coats may prove a winner for you.

What to offer

You will be buying baskets wholesale and then making pillows for them at home to sell together as pet baskets. You will also be making coats for cats and dogs.

What you need

- pet baskets bought wholesale from the manufacturer
- durable, colourful fabric for making cushion covers
- cushion stuffing (polystyrene beads are often used)
- durable, colourful and patterned fabric to make dog and cat coats
- patterns for making dog and cat coats
- trim for fastening the coats
- a sewing machine and thread
- a photo album of happy dogs and cats using their beds and wearing their coats
- a phone and a mobile phone or pager
- business cards, fliers and leaflets detailing your rates and services
- a diary for orders
- a receipt book
- a T-shirt or sweatshirt advertising your business

Getting started

Make up a selection of cat and dog beds. The cushions are easy to make and should fit in the bottom of the basket. Then make up some matching coats to sell as a set. You can also make up a selection of coats to sell separately.

Some unusual suggestions

- a designer pet wetsuit for the dog that loves swimming
- warm pet coats for those cold winters
- pet coats with the dog's name embossed on the side

Dog and cat coats

Dog and cat coats are simple to make. Cut a rectangular piece of fabric the length of the animal's back. At one end, cut out a semi-circle. When you fold the material in half, lengthways, the ends will tie under the cat's or dog's neck. Sew on ties under the neck and under the tummy. You can make up coats for winter or summer – the thicker the layers of material, the warmer they will be. You can even use waterproof material for pets to wear outside on rainy days.

Once you have some samples, try selling them at local markets. Contact neighbourhood vets and ask if they will put a few samples on display, with a flier. If they sell any, see if you can supply them on a regular basis. Put posters up at pet shops or ask the shop owners if they will stock your product. You should also contact dog and cat clubs. Perhaps as a way of promoting the beds or coats you could offer samples of your product as raffle prizes at their next competition.

What to charge

Your prices will depend on your costs for the material and baskets. Try pricing the baskets from around £15. Coats, depending on size and type, should start at around £10. Don't forget you can also do designer wedding coats if the owner decides to take their dog to the happy event.

11 Pet coffins

Don't laugh. We all love our pets dearly and want the best for them. And when devoted owners lose a pet, a coffin or headstone may be what's needed for a proper send-off.

What to offer

You will offer a range of pet coffins and headstones. All your pet products will be handmade and designed with a personal touch.

What you need

- carpentry ability
- chipboard, pine board or other timber
- nails, sander and paint
- access to a branding tool or a wood-burning tool that can burn designs (and letters) into wood
- overalls, gloves and other protective equipment
- business cards
- a portfolio of photographs of coffins and headstones you have designed and constructed
- a phone and a mobile phone or pager
- business cards, fliers and leaflets detailing your rates and services
- a diary
- a receipt book

Getting started

First design and construct some sample coffins and headstones. Then show them to managers of local pet stores and see if they are interested in stocking them. Sell them on the idea of the unique service you offer: the only person locally who designs and makes coffins and headstones for departed cats, dogs, ferrets, birds, mice and other lamented pets. Set up a stall at local markets and take orders. Also contact all cat-, dog- and bird-breeding associations in your area. Tell them about your service. Find out when their show and competition days are on, set up a stall and distribute leaflets. You may even take some orders.

Don't forget to send out a press release about your service to the local media. They may find it just unusual enough to run a story about it.

What to charge

Your price will depend on your wholesale timber costs and the time it takes to make the various products. Start out by setting basic fees for the coffins and the headstones. Here are some examples.

- varnished wooden cross with animal's name burnt in – £15
- coffin for cat or small dog – £25

16

ESPECIALLY FOR TEENAGERS

As a teenager, the pocket money your parents provide is never enough to pay for dates, movies, sporting events, the latest CD, jeans, shirts and other necessities. Because pocket money won't stretch far enough, the only alternative is to make your own.

You can try almost any of the money-making suggestions in this book, or you could try these special teen schemes.

—————— 1 Golf caddy service ——————

If you have an interest in golf you might want to approach local golf clubs and ask if you can offer a golf caddying service to their members for regular weekend competitions or for major tournaments.

To organise regular weekend work, you could put up posters on the club's notice board and in the pro-shop, hand out leaflets and, perhaps, put an advertisement in the club newsletter. If you want to caddy at major tournaments you should ask the golf club to recommend you to contestants or, better still, provide the club with fliers they can include with the tournament entry form.

You need to charge per golf round. Somewhere in the range of £10 is a good starting point.

Important fact

Remember some golf clubs have strict rules governing clothing and who is allowed to caddy and be on the course. Check with the manager or club secretary before you start approaching people.

———— 2 Teen modelling ————

There are many teenagers who dream of becoming a model. It is only the lucky few who succeed but if you would like to try to get work modelling teen clothes for catalogues, TV advertisements or magazines, here are some pointers.

Getting started

You will need to send in a few photos of yourself (head-and-shoulder shots, full length shots) and a CV, detailing your previous experience (if any). Then you need to find a reputable agency.

Be warned!

There are many disreputable agencies in operation, so contact the National Association of Modelling Agents and ask for a list of approved agents. The number can be found in the phone book, or you could try phoning an agency and asking them if they have the association's number.

In the UK the Elisabeth Smith Agency handles children, teens and adults and has a good reputation. Like all agencies it is very busy and may send potential child and teenage models a booklet with information about modelling. The booklet costs around £6 and you need to include a self-addressed label. You can write to the agency at:

Elisabeth Smith Model Agency
81 Headstone Road
Harrow HA1 1PQ

Include a self-addressed stamped envelope for further information. They also have an information line. It is a premium line, so check the current costs. The number is 0891 715393.

Like many such agencies, they are concerned that potential models should not get ripped off or be given the wrong impression about the world of modelling. It is a competitive industry and you must be prepared for long hours of hard work. If you do get accepted by an agency be prepared to go to many casting calls without being chosen. It is hard work so be prepared for some let-downs as well as successes.

Rates

On average children aged from five to twelve can earn up to £60 an hour or up to £300 a day for photographic work. Teens and adults can earn up to £90 an hour or up to £600 a day for photographic work.

Television rates vary and are often negotiated per client. Don't forget that your agency will take a percentage of your fee.

3 Paper delivery

Local newsagents – and sometimes localised newspaper companies – are often on the look-out for young people to deliver newspapers and magazines. Try the direct approach: visit the newsagents and ask them for work. Take a CV if you have one, and some references from teachers or friends. Dress neatly for the interview, so you make a good impression. If you get the job you'll be expected to deliver daily newspapers early in the morning, or perhaps evening papers late in the afternoon. Your employer will let you know whether you need a bicycle or if they provide a trolley.

Delivering weekly papers is different. You will probably have to pick up the papers and deliver them during the day and into the afternoon – the hours are different but it is still hard work.

4 Leaflet distribution

Enterprising teenagers should consider approaching shops and local businesses to ask about doing letter-box drops. The businesses get the leaflets printed, and you walk around the streets, placing leaflets through letter-boxes. You'll need to be fit and have good walking shoes. You will probably get paid by the number of leaflets you deliver. For example, you might be paid £20 to deliver 1000 leaflets. This is the sort of job that a group of teenagers could do together, splitting the area up and offering clients full coverage.

Important fact

Make sure you are working in a safe area and not at night-time by yourself. Your personal safety is important so do not put yourself at risk. Also, make sure you know how and when you are to be paid. There are some employers who take advantage of younger staff so if you have problems tell your parents and ask for their help.

TEACH YOURSELF

SETTING UP A SMALL BUSINESS

Vera Hughes and David Weller

This book is an invaluable guide to setting up and running your own small business. It helps you to identify your product or service and consider the marketing and financing required, and suggests where to go for further advice.

Starting your own business can be a daunting prospect. In addition to helping with the everyday aspects of running a small business, the authors give guidance on specialised areas such as legal requirements, self assessment for income tax, opening a retail or office-based business, staff selection and marketing. 'Key facts' boxes in each chapter give a checklist of important points at each stage.

The authors have been running their own business for several years, and have an abundance of tips and useful information for the entrepreneur.

TEACH YOURSELF

BOOK-KEEPING AND ACCOUNTING
FOR YOUR SMALL BUSINESS
Mike Truman

This clear and practical book provides guidance on how to keep the books and prepare the accounts for your small business. Forget about debits and credits, journal entries, ledgers and day books – if you can read a bank statement this book will teach you how to prepare accounts for tax purposes and for the bank manager, how to make forecasts of your cashflow, and how to prepare a budget for your business.

With completely up-to-date information, the book follows the layout of the new Inland Revenue self-assessment tax return for preparing accounts. Step-by-step coverage of book-keeping and accounting makes this an accessible and invaluable guide for small business needs.

Mike Truman is a Chartered Accountant and a Fellow of the Chartered Institute of Taxation, as well as being a professional writer in accountancy and taxation.

Other related titles

COPYWRITING

J. Jonathan Gabay

You've got the greatest product or service in the world. The trouble is, no one knows about it. Now thanks to this outstandingly informative book, whether you run a small social club, theatrical society, charity or even work for an advertising agency or international organisation, you can soon be writing powerful copy that promises to get your message across.

From planning to implementation *Teach Yourself Copywriting* explodes the mystique surrounding copywriting. In doing so it reveals all the inside secrets that will encourage people to seek out your product or service.

Step-by-step, Jonathan Gabay draws on his wide and extensive experience in advertising and marketing to show you in an entertaining and totally absorbing way how to turn words into the response you need. He covers every aspect of creative advertising and promotion, including:

- radio, TV, press and posters
- direct mail
- the Internet
- business-to-business
- public relations
- recruitment
- charities

Whether you are new to copywriting or already work in an agency or marketing department, this book is indispensable. It is packed from cover to cover with all the facts you need – at your fingertips – to write powerful, compelling copy.